GOSPEL EXPLODED

Reaching the Unreached

BOB MAYO

TRIANGLE

First published in Great Britain in 1996
Triangle
SPCK
Holy Trinity Church
Marylebone Road
London NW1 4DU

British Library Cataloguing-in-Publication Data
A catalogue record of this book is available from
the British Library

ISBN 0-281-04920-3

Typeset by Action Typesetting, Gloucester
Printed in Great Britain by
BPC paperbacks, Aylesbury

To Eddie and Ali – thanks for all your hard work in writing this book with me. It's as much your book as mine.

Contents

Foreword

Halfway through the Decade of Evangelism, there are clear signs that the church is beginning to recognize, though slowly and a bit intermittently, the profound change in mind-set necessary if we are to take with any seriousness the call to share the good news of the saving love of God in Christ Jesus with our whole society. We have begun to acknowledge that the great majority of people in this country are not only not fellow-worshippers, but are actually very ignorant of the Christian faith. Nowhere is this more marked than among young people. Detailed research has shown quite conclusively what all of us knew anyway: that the loss of young people to our church has reached a crisis point. Young people are not hearing the gospel in church because they are not there. And in spite of the best efforts of lawmakers to ensure Christian instruction in the schools, for a variety of reasons this has not often produced an effective transmission of the basics of the Christian story. So there are generations growing up, who simply do not know what the story is.

Bob Mayo and Eddie Webber found themselves working in an area where this was the case. They identified a group of street kids hanging around the street corner, where their church stood, as not 'non-Christian', but *'pre-non Christian'*. That is, as they observed, to be Christian involves choice. But you cannot make that choice if you know nothing of the options. To these youngsters, 'Christ' or 'Jesus' were literally simply swear-words. At the very least, it seemed to Eddie and Bob, the church owed them the information on which to make their choice.

But how to impart that information? For one thing, this was no mere passing on of objective facts, though that was part of it. What had to be transmitted was an experience, of a person, of a relationship of love, that would resonate with the kids' own experience, hopes, dreams, longings. A language had to be found that could compass the glory and wonder of the incarnation, the cross and the resurrection; and yet was the youngsters' own language.

And before there was any hope of breaking through in this way, the people who were doing it had to become credible in the eyes of those kids. This meant those who told the Christian story had to show themselves as bridging the chasm between the wholly alien, felt-to-be-establishment 'churchy' culture within which they stood, and the raw mix of the kids' culture of paganism, sophistication, cultural poverty, tough anti-almost-everything-ism, semi-mysticism: a hard-drinking, drug-ridden world where only a really tough integrity would find acceptance and respect.

In one of the most simple and moving passages in the book we are told how this extraordinary mission got under way:

> Imagine that you are sitting in a church and you hear a sermon about the need to tell people about God. You walk outside at the end of the service and you see a group of young people sitting on the park bench, laughing with each other and drinking cans of lager. As you walk home, you remember the sermon. You think of the young people you saw and you wonder how you could ever talk to them about God. You would feel out of your depth. They might laugh at you. They would not understand what you were saying.
>
> Imagine then that you swallowed all your fear and uneasiness and you invited the young people to

come into a church service with you. What would it
mean for them? What would it mean for you? What
would you say if they smoked or swore in church?
What would you say if they asked you about sex, or
drinking or drugs? How would you talk with them
about the Christian faith?

They did just that. And this book is the story of their
attempt, with all its disasters and all its victories; an
attempt to answer the need to 'tell people about God'.
It is in its own way quite a shocking book: there is no
attempt to sanitize the roughness of this particular
context of evangelism. But it is an heroic book as well,
primarily because of the total commitment of the two
evangelists.

They acknowledge openly all the mistakes that they
made: what is more they say 'sorry'! But they leave us
with two emotions: real sadness that the experiment
came to an end; and a strong hope that they will keep
the conviction that is in them, that emerges in the last
pages, and that they will go back and try again.

For the Gospels tell me that there is almost certainly
more joy in heaven over the couple of rough tough
characters who through this brave experiment came to
call Jesus 'Lord', than over any number of our regular
church offerings of praise. And they also tell me that if
we want to be truly obedient to Jesus when he reminds
us of the 'need to tell people about God', then sitting
in church telling each other the story is not the way to
do it.

For the mind-set now needed in the church is one
which will take us out of the safety zone, to leave the
comfortable (and to the world alien and incomprehen-
sible) 'churchy' culture, and wholly involve ourselves in
our world, whichever bit of it we may happen to
inhabit, for God's sake. So that we may learn the
language and tell the story.

As his former college principal and continuing

friend, I was privileged to be a guest at Bob's wedding, and sat at a table with Eddie. It was a very good image of the heavenly banquet: the total mix, socially, culturally, linguistically; bonded together in delight that grew from a shared experience of the love of Jesus Christ. For the people that I met that day, and particularly Eddie and Bob, there was no awkwardness at all in talking about God; after all, it was because of his love that the mix worked and we could all be there together. Later I was able to follow some of the events in this book as they actually unfolded, including the dreadful grief of the shut-down. (That image of the relentless rain falling, falling, washing it all out, is one of the most powerful in the whole book.)

What this account has done for me is to sharpen my sense of how vital this kind of work must be, and how much support we must give to those who struggle to do it. My prayer is that, inspired by this account, there will be many successors to Bob and Eddie; and that all over Britain, in places where there is simply no knowledge of Christ at all, courageous men and women will risk telling the story in a way the world can hear; though the church find it shocking. For Christ's sake ...

Ruth Etchells

Acknowledgements

Pippa my wife – thank you for marrying me when this all blew up.

I would also like to thank the following people for their support and inspiration – Ruth Etchells, Anne, Pauline, Kath, Kit Martin-Doyle, Michelle, Dave, Kirk, Will Carling, Morag, Guy Sears, Anne, Clive Calver, Snowy and Sybil, Adrian, Kirsty, Alastair, Caroline T, William Tyndale, Caroline A and Richard Cockett.

Thank you to Renee Harding, the oldest member of the church, who wrote to us telling us how much she supported and was praying for the work that we did with the young people.

A special thanks to Joey, Richard, Ricky, Stevey, Stacey, Nicky, Clare, Nicky, Michelle, Carly and everyone else.

1

Eddie Webber and Bob Mayo

In 1408 the constitutions of Oxford forbade the translation of any part of Scripture into English by any man on his own authority under pain of punishment as a heretic. One hundred years later William Tyndale was burnt as a heretic – the first person to translate the Bible into English from the original Hebrew and Greek texts.

Imagine that you are sitting in a church and you hear a sermon about the need to tell people about God. You walk outside at the end of the service and you see a group of young people sitting on the park bench, laughing with each other and drinking cans of lager. As you walk home, you remember the sermon. You think of the young people you saw and you wonder how you could ever talk to them about God. You would feel out of your depth. They might laugh at you. They would not understand what you were saying.

Imagine then that you swallowed all your fear and uneasiness and you invited the young people to come into a church service with you. What would it mean for them? What would it mean for you? What would you say if they smoked or swore in church? What would you say if they asked you about sex, or drinking or drugs? How would you talk with them about the Christian faith?

This book is the story of how Eddie Webber and I, Bob Mayo, did just this and worked with a group of young people in Bermondsey. Our lives before we met and started this work could not have been more different. For myself it was public school and Oxford as I grew up to become an ordained clergyman in the Church of England. For Eddie it was the streets and prison as he grew up to become a professional actor.

In 1987 I was finishing off my upper-middle-class theological education with a couple of years at college in Durham to round off three years as an undergraduate at Oxford. At Oxford I used to go to chapel at Keble College. The services were carefully constructed occasions of powerful ritual and liturgy. I enjoyed the sense of bigness and power and majesty and mystery that the whole thing gave to God.

I was ordained in St Albans Abbey and went to work on a council estate on the edge of Luton. I had glass smashed in front of my garage on some thirty separate occasions; my bathroom window was blown out by an airgun, while I was in the bath. I was propositioned by both men and women. I preached my first sermon, took my first wedding and celebrated my first communion. I baptized, buried and blessed people – hatching, matching and dispatching was the regular rhythm of parish life.

It was hard work. When I left Luton to move to Bermondsey I felt sad because I had loved Luton and had not wanted to leave. I had never heard of Bermondsey, stuck in the shadow of Tower Bridge on the south side of the River Thames in London. I arrived, growling, angry and on edge, to take up the job as the Director of the Cambridge University Mission (CUM, now known as the Salmon Youth Centre), an evangelical youth centre. I was also exhausted. A kid from one of the CUM clubs in Bermondsey said to me soon after I arrived:

'You a vicar?'
'Yes,' I replied.

'What is it like?'

'It is the greatest, most noble most, wonderful thing that anyone could possibly want to do. You find out what God wants you to do and then you do it. There is no higher calling. It is great.'

'I think I'll be a footballer.'

In 1987 Eddie was finishing off his 'working-class' theological education in Wormwood Scrubs. After being a nuisance to the police for a number of years, he had now been falsely charged on fabricated evidence and accused of armed robbery and the attempted murder of the security guard. He was innocent of the charges brought against him. He prayed to God, or whoever might be listening, about this situation: 'Look, God, you know I haven't done anything wrong. I know that I haven't been an angel in my life but surely you can't stand by and let this happen.'

He was facing eighteen years in prison for doing nothing. Confronted with this situation, Eddie reflected on his life. In retrospect he could see that he had wasted a lot of opportunities and that there was a lot more that he wanted to do with his life, like getting involved in music and doing some travelling.

After Eddie had been in prison for two months, his Mum, at home in Bermondsey, was one day looking through some old letters and pulled out one sent by Eddie's brother Jacko, who was also in prison. The letter started: 'What a great visit that was; you and Eddie really cheered up my day.'

For some reason she looked at the date of the letter. It was the same date as the one on which Eddie was supposed to have committed the crimes for which he was in prison. The robbery was committed at 1.30 p.m. in north London but on the same day at 12.00 noon Eddie was stepping off the ferry on the Isle of Wight. He had the ultimate alibi. At the time of the crime of which he was accused, he was visiting his brother and had signed his name in the prison visitors' book. On the way to the prison he had taken a taxi and he had left a book in the back of the taxi. Not only did the taxi-driver remember giving him a ride but he still had the book at home.

All charges against Eddie were dropped. He was released from prison and went to Israel, where he got into a bit of music. He stayed in Israel for eleven months and toured in a band. He came home to London and when his band split up, he decided that he would be an actor. He went to college and took a drama course. At the audition for the drama course, he met Ali. They both got on to the course and struck up a friendship.

One day they were talking in Ali's flat about Jesus. Eddie's view was that Jesus was a con man with twelve other very clever people around him. They had got together and exploited a totally illiterate race for their own benefit. Ali disagreed and put across the idea that Jesus had either been God, a lunatic or a liar. Ali believed that Jesus was God. Eddie went home and read the Bible, trying to find something negative about Jesus to prove his theory and to come back at Ali. He could not find anything suggesting that Jesus was a lunatic or a liar and if Jesus had not been a lunatic or a liar, then he must have been a sane man and telling the truth. The next night Eddie rang up Ali and told her, 'I have said some very bad things about Jesus. If I say sorry and ask him to come into my heart, do you think that he will?'

Ali was amazed because they had never once spoken about becoming a Christian and yet here was Eddie on the end of the phone understanding completely about the need for repentance. Eddie's knowledge was a revelation from God rather than an explanation from Ali or other Christians. It was instinct from inside him rather than information from outside that was direct-ing him towards God.

Eddie had worked through the reality of God without churches, without explanations and without theological concepts. Our work was to be motivated by the desire to make God as real as this to the young people in Bermondsey. All the work that we did focused on the one central question – when someone knows nothing about Christ or Christianity, what do we need to do and say in order to get them interested and involved? How could we create an atmosphere where young people from Bermondsey, who knew little or nothing about Christ, could come and get to know Christ in an environment to which they could relate? How could we provide an opportunity for them to worship God, to hear the stories from the Bible and to pray?

Eddie wrote a prayer and put it to music. It echoed through everything that we did together. CUM was a youth club in Bermondsey run by paid staff and volunteers for the young people. I was the Director and Eddie was on the staff as an evangelist. St James' was the parish church where we worshipped and where we believed that God wanted us to root our work with the young people. Bringing the young people into the church building was a key part of the original vision.

> Father in heaven hear our prayer
> As we ask upon our bended knee
> Father in heaven hear our prayer
> Make tight our bonds to you and set us free.
>
> Give us your words that we may speak
> Give us your power so we're not weak
> Show us to be just like your Son
> Who died on the cross to make us one.
>
> Father in heaven we will proclaim
> With our bodies, minds and souls
> Father in heaven we will proclaim
> Through Jesus Christ we will be whole.

Give us your light that burns so bright
Help us to see in darkest night
Give us your truth to build your church
And show us the way to end our search.

Father in heaven hear our prayer
As we ask upon our bended knee
Father in heaven hear our prayer
Make tight our bonds to you and set us free
Make tight our bonds to you and set us free
Make tight our bonds to you and set us free.

2

Clocking in and Clocking off

I defy the Pope and all his laws, if God spare my life, ere many years I will cause a boy that driveth the plough shall know more of the Scripture than thou dost.

(William Tyndale)

Eddie had only been a Christian for four months and had been working with a group of Muslim young people at his church in west London. He was confused about what he was doing there, knowing that he wanted to do something with young people but not sure what. He was praying to God and God told him that what he was doing with the young people in west London he could be doing with the kids in Bermondsey, where he was born and bred.

A couple of months after having this vision from God and once Eddie was convinced that God was telling him to start a service at St James', the local parish church, he went to the then curate, Snowy Davoll. Twenty years previously Snowy had been doing my job as Director of CUM and had known Eddie as a club member, who would think nothing of pulling up in a stolen car and wreaking havoc in the club. Now here was Eddie on his doorstep saying that he had some work to do for God. The conversation between the two of them was short and to the point:

'Snow, I think that God is telling me to start up a service for young kids.'
'Right ... When do you want to start it?'

'This Sunday.'

Snowy suggested that Eddie shared his vision with the rest of the church and when he stood up in St James', where I had been worshipping since my arrival from Luton six months earlier, and talked about how he had a vision from God to start a service in church specifically geared towards young people in Bermondsey, I listened with interest. They were the same young people with whom I was beginning to work in my capacity as Director at CUM. At the end of the service I went up and introduced myself. This was the beginning of our work together.

The existing structures of the church are geared round believing Christians rather than non-believing young people. What we were to recognize was that these existing structures were a barrier to these young people coming to God. The young people were open to the figure of Christ but they were put off by the role of the church. We felt frustrated because we thought that the message of Christ was being complicated by systems and structures, rules and regulations. We felt excited because we thought that we could do something about it.

In the film, *The Blues Brothers*, actors Dan Akroyd and John Belushi have a mission from God to get together a band in order to do a gig and raise five thousand dollars, to pay the tax bill on the orphanage where they grew up. All they have is their 'shades, a full tank of juice and a mission from God'. Our theology was no more complicated than that – 'shades, full tank of juice, trust God, give it a go and see what happens.' Through trial and error we learnt to put aside preconceived notions about God, Christ, salvation, the church or anything else traditionally associated with the label of Christianity.

The young people had no notion of Jesus as a human being. Hanging up on the wall inside St James above the altar is a twenty-foot picture of the resurrected Jesus floating in the clouds. When we asked them what they thought Jesus was like they just pointed at the picture. This was the Jesus that the church was presenting to the young people and it did not mean anything to them; they could not relate to it at all.

I had worked abroad as a missionary with the Church of South India. The most basic idea that I had drummed into me was the idea that no one should impose an interpretation of Christianity on anyone else, but instead people should be allowed to develop their own understanding of God. I had it hammered into me that the people I would meet in India had their own culturally relevant forms of Christianity. Ten years after coming back from India, I was learning to apply the same 'missionary critique' to work in my own country with young people in Bermondsey.

In order to present Jesus in a way that they could understand we started to break down the myth of Jesus as an untouchable God-like creature in order to build up the reality of Jesus as a human being on earth. They thought that if Jesus trod on a nail, it would not hurt him because he was God. If we could not convey to them his humanity and suffering, then what was the point of Jesus coming down to earth to be an example to us?

I had spent seven years preparing for my ordination and three years working at a church in Luton. Now in Bermondsey, Eddie was teaching me how little we actually knew about Jesus besides what was usually taught in a church. What we had been taught in church did not satisfy our curiosity and if it did not satisfy us then it was not going to satisfy the young people. There is a lot to getting to know Jesus. There is the Jesus that Peter had known for three years – eating, drinking, sleeping, tired, depressed, happy and excited – and there was the Jesus that Paul had known who had knocked him out and blinded him on the road to Damascus. Peter's

Jesus was the oppressed, human Jesus and Paul's Jesus was the powerful, supernatural Jesus.

What was Jesus like as a human being? Would he have sat forward listening intently to what was being said or would he have sat back letting the conversation flow around him? Would he have been witty and talkative or would he have been the strong and silent type? What were his idiosyncrasies? Did he squint? What amused him? What excited him? Once we started asking these questions we had something that interested us as much as it interested the young people – the realities of the bearded, sandalled, oppressed Jesus on earth.

The disciples did not worship the Jesus in heaven until they had spent three years with the Jesus on earth. In church we worship the Jesus in heaven because, as Christians, we accept the reality of Jesus' time on earth. The young people did not accept the reality of Jesus' time on earth; therefore the Jesus in heaven meant nothing to them. We needed to introduce the young people to the Jesus on earth before we could ask them to consider Jesus in heaven.

They were not used to this approach and were startled when we talked about Jesus with teeth black with dirt, or Jesus with body odour because he had not washed for three days. It caught their attention because it deconstructed the squeaky clean, holier-than-thou, halo-wearing Jesus that they had in their imaginations. It built up a picture of Jesus as a real human being. Even the basic fact that he was not English startled the young people. Because of a deep-seated prejudice towards ethnic minorities in Bermondsey, if Jesus had walked in the room then they might have slagged him off (insulted him) as a black man.

We needed to keep our thoughts simple and logical. Everything we did was hard and once we were aware that it was always going to be so then we were on our way. The important thing for me was that I did not try to be clever or academic. We started the service off very simply by gathering together people to play in a music group and beginning to find and work out songs.

We developed the music group and six months later we held our first service. Only Christians came. Eddie and I looked at each other and shook our heads. We knew that this was not the vision. We prayed to God: 'This was meant to be a youth service, God. If you want us to do this work stop sending committed Christians to the service and send us the young people instead.'

It was some months before our prayer was answered but one Sunday we went to the church and found a group of young people outside, drinking and smoking. Eddie went up and asked them to come into church.

'What for?'
'To hear about God.'

They laughed. We went inside. Ten minutes later they walked into the church while we were worshipping. That was the start of the vision as we knew it and it marked the beginning of a hectic and exciting piece of work. One year later the service was shut down. It was just before Christmas and we faced a crowd of thirty-five young people, milling about aimlessly outside the church confused and annoyed: 'Why are you shutting our service? Why don't you shut the service for them?' they shouted, pointing at the people going in for the early evening worship.

So what happened between clocking in and clocking off?

3
Evangelism

> Evangelion (that we call the gospel)... This is a Greek word and signifieth good, merry, glad and joyful tidings, that maketh a man's heart glad, and maketh him sing, dance and leap for joy.
>
> *(William Tyndale)*

Urgency and anger motivated a lot of our work with the young people. We felt clear that 'knowing Jesus' was something beautiful and if people were prevented from knowing Christ by systems, something was horribly wrong. We wanted to get to the young women before they got pregnant and to the young men before they ended up in prison.

In my perception, there are three divides. There are Christians. There are 'non-Christians' and there are 'pre-non Christians'. Non-Christians are people who have had contact with church or Christians and have some understanding of the framework of Christianity. The reason that they are not Christians is either hostility, apathy or disagreement.

'Pre-non Christians' are people who have little or no knowledge or understanding of Christ or Christianity. Jesus is a word to be used negatively – it is nothing more than a swear-word. The reason that they are not Christians is not hostility, apathy or disagreement but ignorance of the basic Christian stories.

Traditionally the church has worked with non-Christians. Until recently most of the country have been non-Christians and the reality of the pre-non Christian is not yet catered for in the church's thinking. Pre-non Christianity is a comparatively recent development. These days there is less Christian education in schools; only seven per cent of the population go to church and now it is the grandparents, and not the parents, who know any of the Bible stories. Most of the young people with whom we worked were pre-non Christians, and there was no church structure able to provide appropriate teaching and nurture for them. No one taught us about it. We had to work it out for ourselves.

I felt that I was stumbling on a great discovery when I worked out the distinctions between Christians, non-Christians and pre-non Christians. I was told by committed thinking Christians that the concept of pre-non Christianity was inspired and could be a valuable tool in unlocking the gospel to many people. However, this reaction was in itself a tragedy. I recently gave a presentation to a group of research students, most of whom were not Christians. I explained to them this so-called discovery of pre-non Christianity. I was excited and enthusiastic. I was met with silence. Some commented, 'Are you blind? Have you only just realized that?' It was embarrassing that an idea considered exciting by Christians was seen by non-believers as being so basic that it was not worth mentioning.

Eddie's and my task was to solder the divide between the Christian and the pre-non Christian. We needed to get into a position where a pre-non Christian and a Christian could listen to each other and discuss the Bible constructively. We needed to reach the pre-non Christians living in a world of pre-non Christians and explain to them the supernatural workings of Christ.

What I had to learn was that enabling pre-non Christian young people to learn about God was something very different to teaching Christians or non-Christians. The pre-non Christian's learning is like the microwave. The teaching for the Christians is like the oven. Think of the difference between how a microwave and an oven cook a chicken. A microwave cooks a chicken from the inside out and an oven cooks a chicken from the outside in.

Think of the difference between having cancer and reading about the effects of cancer. When you have cancer you have experienced what is involved and have felt the effects. When you read about cancer you have a theoretical understanding of the effects of cancer but you do not know what it feels like.

Think of the difference between knowing Jesus and listening to information about Jesus. To know Jesus truly you need to know him organically. Organic knowledge is knowledge from within, relying on instincts, feelings and common sense and feeding on experiences rather than information. When you only have information about Jesus your knowledge is based on what you have been told rather than what you have experienced for yourself.

If you put the chicken in the oven with the temperature too high, the outside will get burnt but the inside will remain raw. If you give too much information about Jesus to the young people then it does not mean anything to them. They cannot relate to it. If we are not teaching the young people to know Jesus organically then what we are teaching is useless to them. They need to know Jesus organically in order for Jesus to make sense in their lives.

If knowledge is God-inspired and organic, it grows naturally and can reach conclusions by itself. When the young people first came into our service twenty of them were smoking. Jean, the cleaner, was going mad because she had to clear up all the fag-ends on Monday morning. Four months passed; five of them decided that it was wrong to smoke in the church and told the others to stop smoking. We said nothing. The young people had 'evangelized' each other.

Organic knowledge came when the young people were able to experience Christ before they were required to understand him. 'Christians pray' is information; saying 'try talking to God yourself' is using an organic approach. 'Christians worship in church' is information; suggesting 'come and sing' is using an organic approach.

Salvation was a concept that the young people did not understand. 'Do not have sex outside marriage' was an instruction that they were not going to obey. 'Come to church on Sunday morning' was something that they were not going to do. However, the fact that they did not understand salvation, the fact that they were going to have sex and the fact that they were not going to come to church on Sunday mornings did not mean that we could not teach them about Jesus. I had been taught that discovering Jesus followed on from understanding Jesus. By contrast, what we taught the young people was that understanding follows on from discovery. If we had insisted on explaining everything and not moving forward until they understood everything, we would have been putting blocks in their path towards understanding Jesus.

The young people needed information; enough to inform their choice but not too much to stifle their thinking. For example, the fact that Jesus got angry might stimulate the young people's thinking. The fact that Jesus got angry but remained without sin because he was the Son of God might stifle their thinking because it would leave them confused. It would re-assure a Christian or even a non-Christian to hear someone speaking about Jesus being the Son of God and without sin, because they would know the context in which it was said. It would confuse a pre-non Christian, however, because they would have no knowledge of that context.

Organic knowledge is self-generating, feeding on itself rather than constantly looking for external input.

If we read three books on joy and simply kept what we read as theoretical understanding then we would need to keep on reading books in order to refresh our knowledge. If we experienced joy, we would not need to read a book about it. If we listened to three sermons on the meaning of forgiveness and kept what we had heard as theoretical understanding then we would need to listen to a fourth sermon, again in order to refresh our knowledge. If we truly experienced forgiveness then we would not need the sermons.

The best bit of God and, as far as the young people were concerned, the only bit of God worth having was the freedom of God. They did not experience this in church on Sunday mornings – stand up, sit down, say a prayer, keep quiet, sing a song, and so on. To the young people it felt as if there was within the church service a sign saying 'keep off the grass' and signs saying 'keep off the grass' are always put on the best bits of grass. What we taught the young people was that the freedom of God was the best bit of grass and that they could walk on the grass and enjoy it – let the young people dance, let them make a noise, let them sit down when they want, stand up when they want. Who cares what they are doing as long as they are learning about God? Our Sunday evening services were intended to cater for this approach.

There were a number of Christians who came to the service and were very excited by what we were doing. Caroline had been going to church for some years and she began coming along on Sunday evenings to see what was happening. She was a live-in volunteer working with the young people at CUM. She found herself challenged by what was going on in the service – energy, laughter, spark and noise – and wondered why she had never been fired by the same enthusiasm. She was used to church as a duty and not as fun. She enjoyed the spontaneity of what we were doing and was challenged by the sincerity of the young people worshipping God.

She had a dream. In the dream she was asleep and someone was encouraging her to wake up. She talked about it with me. She felt that the dream was Jesus telling her to wake up and that her years of going to church had been like sleepwalking. In other words, her knowledge of Jesus had been based on received information rather than on anything organic. We prayed together and she committed her life to Christ. It was an encouragement to us that the service was affecting people in different ways and that she had recognized that God was apparent in the work that we were doing with the young people.

We needed to develop teaching methods that would draw young people into an understanding of God. We knew that the wrong approach would put them off. No one goes up to a group of Millwall football supporters and tells them that they should support Chelsea. The only effect would be to make them more firm in their commitment to Millwall and more set in a dislike of Chelsea. We were not going to tell the young people that they had to become Christians or else they would go to hell. We were not denying that this might not be the reality of the situation, but we needed to find the right way to say it.

Do we really understand what the different pictures of hell in the Bible mean? Are the pictures literal or symbolic? Manufactured images of devils wearing red cloaks and prodding us with forks were not much use in terms of getting the young people interested in Christianity. They were as abstract as the idea of God as an old man with a beard, and heaven being a place where everyone dresses in white, plays harps and smiles at each other. Do we really think that the devil has a red suit and a tail anyhow? We did not want to lay false and abstract concepts on the young people that would not help them to understand the reality of God.

The Bible's teaching on hell conjures up images of people in agony and frustration for eternity – it is not a pretty picture and neither should it be! If there is a one per cent chance that one per cent of these images have one per cent of the truth in them about what happens when people die, then it makes the whole issue of heaven and hell terrifying. To the young people, however, it turned the concept of heaven and hell into a farce by making it all too big and too supernatural. The young people to whom we talked lived within the realms of reality and from their perspective hell was a lot more interesting than heaven. One person's comment was: 'I would rather go to hell because at least I will be down there with all my mates. At least in hell you can have a drink, have a joint and have a good rump (sexual intercourse).' They did not want to go to heaven where everyone was good and perfect and smiled all the time.

What we did was to talk to the young people about heaven and hell in ways that were relevant to their everyday living. We used simple illustrations, not to provide definitive explanations but to get them thinking. For example:

'Why does it say that I will not get to heaven if I do not know Jesus?' Nicky asked.

I replied, 'Put it this way. Someone goes to your Mum's house, knocks on the door and asks for food. Your Mum does not know who she is. Will your Mum let her into the house and feed her?'

'No.'

'But what if you met someone? You find out that the person is hungry. You then go with her to your Mum and you ask your Mum to give her some food. Will your Mum let her into the house and feed her then?'

'Yes.'

'It is the same with God. If you turn up at heaven and God does not know who you are, he will not let you in. However, if Jesus turns up with you and tells God that you are a friend of his then God will let you in and give you something to eat.'

We talked about hell in terms of what happened here and now and we used that as a comparison. God has got his kingdom in heaven and the devil has got his kingdom here on earth. We talked about heaven and earth rather than heaven and hell. We told them that they would not have to wait until they died to understand hell. Hell could be here on earth. Working with this idea we could explain the idea of hell in a way that anyone could understand.

The young people had met both Ali, now Eddie's wife, and Pippa, my wife. They liked and admired both of them and so when we equated hell with what we would feel like if we had an affair they listened.

'Neither Eddie nor I are going to be unfaithful to our wives partly because of what it would do to them but also because of what it would do to us – our hell would be knowing what we had done wrong. Jesus could have walked away from all that he had to do but would he have been able to live with himself if he had done so? That would have been his earthly hell. Physical pain is one thing but mental or emotional pain is far worse.'

The one thing that all the young people understood was the idea that nothing was easy. They knew that life was difficult and tough. They understood suffering more than they understood pleasantness and happiness and they were not going to be persuaded by us telling them that if they become a Christian then everything would be rosy and all right. We felt that Jesus never pretended that being a Christian would be anything other than hard. He says that if you want to get to heaven you have got to go through the narrow door, which is about five foot high and three foot wide; not only that, you have to drag a great ten-foot cross weighing a ton through it as well.

What we said to the young people was: 'If you think

that things are difficult it is nothing compared to how difficult they might be when you are a Christian.'

Eddie said that he found it harder being a Christian than anything that he had known before. His story was not a standard 'repented sinner seeing the light and turning from the error of his ways' type account. Before he was a Christian he did what he wanted. It was fun. After he became a Christian he was introduced into a world of 'shoulds' and 'oughts' and 'do's' and 'don'ts'.

Eddie taught me that in Bermondsey, authority is nothing and respect is everything. Nobody gets respect automatically; you have to earn it. I found that when there was a sense of give and take and discussion then I began to earn that respect. Kirk, at seventeen, was a pre-non Christian young person drawn into the work that we were doing. He was a bit of a warrior – black belt at karate, often drunk and getting into fights, the big man, who would be drawn into finishing off fights for other people. He came with us when we took a group of young people, with whom we had been working in our evening service, away for a weekend near Weybridge in rural Surrey. Everyone involved in the worship group and those who helped with the service came with us. As far as we knew, during the weekend, Kirk did not express any response to what we were saying and what we were doing. After the weekend we had little contact with him for two years other than the occasional hello in the street.

What we did not know and what we did not find out until we met up with him again at the fair which comes to Bermondsey once a year, was that he was working through Christianity in his head and coming to conclusions for himself.

Kirk was standing by the amusement arcade, lager in hand, smile on his face, watching the world go by. He told us about how he 'got into God' (his words) during our weekend at Weybridge. He told us about the time when he and I went out canoeing and how he ended up exhausted. He was a fit lad who worked out in the gym and he was surprised to be out-canoed. After lunch that day we had had a water fight. I had ended up face down in the river with my feet waving in the air. Something had clicked in him. It was a laugh. The relaxed atmosphere meant that when Eddie suggested to Kirk that he tried talking to God Kirk saw it as a suggestion rather than a challenge. He saw it as an idea to be considered rather than a command to be obeyed or ignored. When Eddie had told him to talk to God he decided that he would give it a try; there was no profound conversion at this stage – it was just a case of 'why not?' The weekend had enabled him to realize that he could get to know Jesus without losing his identity and he was seeing Eddie, whom he had known long before Eddie became a Christian, standing up and talking about God.

We asked ourselves what had been so special about the weekend that had left Kirk so powerfully affected. On the journey there the young people had still looked upon me as the traditional 'do this and don't do that' Bible-bashing Christian. Through the work at the church and through CUM the young people had come into contact with a number of Christians. It had not taken long for them to form an impression of Christians as people, who would tell them how to behave and who would tell them what was right and what was wrong. We knew how they thought and we knew that we needed to break down this understanding of Christians. When we arrived we could not find the keys and they were very angry with us for losing them. After a while I found the keys in one of the bags but did not tell anyone. I kept people looking for another hour. Everyone got even more angry; Eddie was more wound up than anyone. After an hour I said that we should pray for the keys to be found; we prayed and I promptly produced them out of my pocket. They were furious and Eddie especially so.

The point of it was that in their eyes I was still the traditional, conceptual, churchy Christian. They did not expect me to wind them up by pretending that I had lost the keys. I needed to deconstruct their image of what a Christian was and to clear away the perceptions they had of Christianity so that they would work things out for themselves. In the eyes of the young people Eddie was one of them and not a traditional, conceptual, churchy Christian. They gave me respect because Eddie gave me respect but that could only take me so far. I needed to break through the labels that they had put on me and establish the fact that the common denominator between the two of us was God.

We were two people with God at the forefront of our lives. We did not have to keep ramming God down their throats because they knew that what we did was done in the context of God. We had worked with them in the church for the previous eight or nine months and so they knew what we believed. We went down to Weybridge to enjoy ourselves with no plans and no structures. The youth work and evangelism textbooks were nowhere to be seen – Eddie started a water fight at two o'clock in the morning because no one would go to sleep; we took beers and chopped down trees for firewood. Before we went, we said to each other that if discussions and Bible readings came out of it then that would be a bonus. We had a lot of bonuses that weekend – natural, spontaneous and unplanned, such as reading the Bible by candlelight at three o'clock in the morning.

It worked for Kirk and it meant a lot to all of the young people. A lot of seeds were sown without our knowledge. Kirk was up in court a few months after the weekend. He was charged with beating up his teacher and was facing a prison sentence. He prayed to God for help. To everyone's, and especially his own, relief and surprise he was acquitted, and walked out of court without going to jail. He put two and two together – the weekend and praying to God and he gave God the credit for giving him another chance. Kirk said to us that every time he went on the bus or was in the street he was given a leaflet about God by a street evangelist. He was very confused because this had never happened to him before. As soon as he committed his life to God, however, he was not given another tract. We reckoned that God must have wanted Kirk badly because he was prepared to move in extraordinary ways to get him.

As he got to know God, Kirk was able to recognize what had actually been happening in his life before. What he realized was that he had been used by people because he was big and powerful and useful to have around. People wanted him to help when they were fighting and, if necessary, finish off the fights for them. The result was that he kept getting arrested by the police. Kirk was not going to tell the police who it was that had started the fight. 'Thou shalt not "grass" (inform)' is the eleventh commandment in Bermondsey. He might have gained respect for not grassing but it was respect that he could do without. It was costing him money. He would end up with a £200 fine.

'Getting into God' for Kirk meant staying off drugs, being faithful to his girlfriend and not getting involved in these fights and, as a result of this, keeping out of prison. Church and reading the Bible and going to prayer meetings were not things that he could relate to at this stage.

He might not have been in church but he was talking about God in places that the churches were not reaching, witnessing in his home environment. He was struggling to work out God in every area of his life and as he struggled, he was talking. He talked to someone at his snooker club.

'Do you believe in God?' Kirk asked.
'You aren't one of those religious nutters, are you?'

the person replied. 'I used to be a choir boy but I don't believe in God any more. Is he going to help me to pocket that ball?'

'Don't mock', said Kirk. 'If you mock you must think that God exists because you can't mock something that is not there.'

We knew what Kirk was going through because Eddie told me that he had been through exactly the same experiences. When Eddie started learning about Christianity he needed to work out God before he could work out Jesus. Eddie considered Jesus to be a harder concept to grasp than God. God in heaven, big and powerful, is a straightforward idea. God on earth, as a human being crucified, is much more complicated. Eddie had been making his money from all sorts of illegal sources. There were certain things such as handling cannabis that he knew were wrong, and when he became a Christian, he stopped doing them. There were other things that he did not stop doing – having sex before marriage, having the odd joint and swearing. This did not fit into the church's approach. The church has a clearly defined moral culture with everything already worked out – you should not have sex before marriage; you should not smoke cannabis; you should not swear. The result is that there is nowhere for people like Eddie or Kirk to work things through for themselves without either being made to feel uncomfortable or being made to feel guilty. Eddie and Kirk needed to develop an independent relationship with God before they could work out the 'do's' and 'don't s' of the religion.

Some years before working in Bermondsey, I ran a night shelter for homeless young people in Oxford. There was room for no more than twelve people to stay the night, and there were two different schools of thought about how the shelter should operate. One thought was to restrict the number of people staying to twelve and to allow them to stay for only three nights in order to ensure a turnover of people. My approach was to allow any number of people into the shelter and to allow them to stay for more than three nights. This meant that when the night shelter became crowded, people would decide for themselves about moving on.

Eddie had been to a church service where the vicar invited anyone to come to the front of the church and talk about their experiences of God. Two people came to the front and spoke. A third person was making her way up to the front when the vicar stopped her and went on to the next part of the service. The vicar wanted to move the service on because he knew that the woman spoke in church whenever there was an opportunity, and he felt that she would not have anything to say. Eddie wanted to be allowed to draw that conclusion for himself. He did not want the vicar to do his thinking for him. How was anyone to know that God was not going to speak through the woman that particular week?

My conviction as to how the night shelter should be run and Eddie's reaction to the vicar stopping the woman from speaking at the front of the church fed into our realization that the Bible became more alive when people were allowed to interpret it for themselves. Christianity became accessible to people like Kirk if they were given the space and the opportunity to think issues through for themselves rather than being dictated to as to what was right and what was wrong. God will convict people over what is right and what is wrong once they have an independent relationship with him.

When Kirk asked a Christian about why Jesus had been crucified he was told that there was God on one side, there was man on the other side and there was sin in the middle. The death of Jesus bridged the gap between God and man by taking the sin on himself. This was a traditional conceptual Christian explanation of the crucifixion and it was quite useless to someone like Kirk. He had spent two years organically working through Christianity on his own and getting to know God. It had taken a Christian twenty minutes to confuse him totally. He had wanted milk and he had been given a piece of steak. All he had wanted to know was the fact that the crucifixion was the Roman method of execution and that the Jews had conspired to put Jesus to death. In Kirk's language Jesus had been 'fitted up'.

If time and space and support are not available for people to develop an independent relationship with God, the church sets up a dependency culture. As long as Kirk was given enough information to help him work out the Christian faith at his own speed, then his new life in Christ was something generic and organic growing inside him. As soon as he was given too much information that did not make sense to him and needed explaining, he became dependent on other people to explain the explanations.

The Bible teaches how important it can be to work things out for ourselves rather than being solely dependent on what others tell us. When Paul had a vision on the road to Damascus he was a highly educated man knowing the Jewish law in detail. After his vision he had no contact with anyone else and went away to the desert for three years before returning to Jerusalem (Galatians 1.17–18). He had to work out the implications of the vision for himself. In the Old Testament, Jeremiah worries about how the Israelites will worship God with the temple in ruins and everyone in exile. He foresees a time when 'there will not be any teachers because everyone will know God for themselves.' (Jeremiah 31.34).

I worked in Madras in south India for two years after my years at university and during that time I worked in a team that shared a responsibility for five villages. As we could not be in each of the five villages every week, we paid a Hindu girl to read from the Scriptures at the same time and in the same place each week. Then we would visit each village every sixth week and we would find groups of people already sitting round discussing the stories that they had heard. We found that the Christian stories did not need explanation in order to make them interesting. The explanations could come after people's interest had been aroused. This was the approach that we used with the pre-non Christian young people in Bermondsey when we taught them that understanding would follow discovery of Jesus.

When Jesus was asked 'Who then is my neighbour?' (Luke 10.29) he told the story of the Good Samaritan and left his listeners to work out the implications for themselves. When his disciples asked him why he talked in parables, Jesus replied, 'To those on the outside everything is said in parables so that, "they may be ever seeing but never perceiving, and ever hearing but never understanding; otherwise they might turn and be forgiven"' (Mark 4.12). By its very nature the word of God was too powerful to be absorbed all at once and if people were interested enough to want to know more, they would come and ask Jesus and he would explain the story to them. His approach to teaching was to throw the weight of responsibility on to those who listened and leave them to approach him and ask what he meant.

What about the man called Legion that Jesus healed by sending the evil spirits into the herd of swine? He was desperate to remain with Jesus but Jesus sent him away telling him to go back to his people and tell them what had happened. Not a word of explanation about the fact that his cure was a part of the messianic fulfil-ment longed for by the people of Israel. Not a word of explanation about the fact that it was the Son of God who had healed him. All Jesus said was: 'Go and tell people what has happened.' Work it out for yourself. Put the word around something is going on.

What about the rich young ruler? Jesus looked at him

with sadness in his eyes because he was so close to the kingdom of heaven. However, Jesus did not follow after him and try to persuade him to give away all he had to the poor. Jesus made no attempt to try and explain how he has not quite got things right. Jesus turned and watched him walk away.

What about the virgins outside the wedding feast? 'We have not got enough oil', they say to the other women waiting with them for the bridegroom's return. 'Tough', say the other women, 'we are not going to give you any of our spare oil because our lamps might run out and then we would be in trouble. If you have not got any oil then it is your problem.' The women go off to get some oil and miss the arrival of the bridegroom. There is nothing sentimental about Christianity – it involves a tough, practical approach to life.

If evangelism is only something that we do rather than something of who we are, it may end up being over-structured and forced rather than something spontaneous and natural. If it is not natural, it is not real. If it is not real, then it is not good news to anyone; not to us and not to the young people.

In the world where the young people lived you tried something and took the consequences. The culture in Bermondsey does not hold the kids to a system – 'you do what you do when you do it'. I was having Sunday lunch. A little hand appeared in the window. Someone was trying to break in. Another hand appeared and then a head appeared. He looked round and saw us sitting down and having our food. 'Sorry, mate', he said very politely and disappeared.

On another occasion my parents had come for Sunday lunch. There was a knock on the door. Someone had been trying to break in and was now stuck on the roof. Could I bring a ladder and get him down? There was nothing 'personal' in him trying to break in. He tried. It did not work and now he was needing help. The young people's culture was to rely

on their instincts and to work things out for themselves
– think fast, think on your feet and think for yourself.
In order to connect with this approach to life, to teach
them about God, we needed a spontaneous, unstruc-
tured atmosphere that made itself up around what
everyone wanted to do. Initial knowledge about God,
organically learnt, would grow naturally and without a
dependency upon continual church input.

Things can get worse when people start getting to
know God. Some years previously I had worked with
one couple, where the wife was a Christian and was
praying for her husband to become a Christian. She
and I were both thrilled when her prayers were
answered and he committed his life to God. However,
what happened was that they ended up divorced. He
said that it was only after he became a Christian that
he was able to recognize how bad his marriage really
was.

It was in order to have integrity in what we were
doing that we taught the young people that becoming a
Christian could make things harder for them, but we
also taught them that it was an adventure and that it
was exciting.

The angels might rejoice over a repentant sinner –
let them; they are in heaven. We are down here on
earth and this is reality. Becoming a Christian is great
but what happens next – the journey once you have
become a Christian – can be painful and hard. The
reality of becoming a Christian is that not only do you
have the devil against you, but you have your own
people against you. You are going to get knocked down
and you have to get up; and then you get knocked
down again, and then you get knocked down again;
and then you get knocked down again. When someone
becomes a Christian it is 'welcome to the fight'. As in
the film, *Terminator*, where the humans are fighting
against powerful machines, you shake hands, looking
the new recruit in the eyes, feeling glad that he is

joining in but feeling at the same time sad that he is now a part of the suffering. What keeps you going is knowing the truth and having the power of God behind you.

4

Sex

> Nevertheless in translating the New Testament I did my
> duty, and so do I now, and will do as much as God hath
> ordained me to do ... If God's word bear record unto it
> and thou feelest in thine heart that it be so, be of good
> comfort and give God thanks.
>
> *(William Tyndale)*

Our attitudes towards sex and marriage are determined
by culture and upbringing as well as by conviction and
belief. I grew up in the public school environment with
'all boys together' and sex was a taboo subject. Eddie
grew up in a working-class environment with boys and
girls together and sex a natural and accepted part of
the culture. Sex has different connotations in a middle-
class as opposed to a working-class culture. For a
middle-class woman with a stifled family background,
saying 'yes' to sex can be freedom. For a working-class
woman with a difficult family background saying 'no' to
sex can be freedom.

What were we going to say about sex in an environment where sex was a totally accepted part of life?
People had sex just to relieve their boredom. Kids
sometimes lost their virginity at eleven and were mums
and dads at sixteen. Sex was on television, in pop songs,
in advertisements, in magazines. Every medium
directed towards the young people involved sex.

The only teaching that I received on sex through a
church was: 'Do not have sexual intercourse outside

marriage.' I found that this teaching could be a block to people getting to know Jesus and also to Christians because it could leave them feeling guilty and inadequate when they found they could not live up to the teaching, even in their minds. It could be a block to pre-non Christians because marriage is a social and economic issue as well as a moral and Christian issue. If someone cannot afford the expense of a wedding or cannot afford to lose their income support and benefits for single people, they are more likely to live together than marry.

We found that teaching the young people not to have sexual intercourse outside marriage, without building up a more developed understanding of Jesus, was putting the cart before the horse. It was as if we were saying, 'Because you don't have sex outside marriage, you will get to know Jesus' rather than 'Because you know Jesus, you will choose not to have sex outside marriage.'

I used to go to church on Sundays desperately trying to keep my sexual urges in check, and feeling thoroughly guilty about trying but failing to live up to the teachings about sex that I was hearing from the pulpit. Sex is such a powerful issue that if it is not treated with compassion, people end up feeling guilty and no one learns anything about God by feeling guilty. Jesus died to take away our guilt, so why do Christians get so wound up over sex? We found that doing nothing other than teaching that sexual intercourse should be kept within marriage was an inadequate treatment of this issue, because it made the main issue whether or not people slept together rather than whether or not they learnt anything about Christ. We would talk with the young people about using condoms. We would give them advice on sex. The main purpose of what we were doing, however, was not to teach them life skills but to teach them about Jesus. We knew that in learning about Jesus, and living with Jesus, he would convict them far more effectively than we could, of what was the 'right' and what was the 'wrong' thing for them to do.

The one recurring theme to our work was how we could make Christ accessible and relevant to the young people. There was no other question that motivated us. If there was anything that prevented the young people from coming into contact with Jesus, we wanted to clear it away.

Some of the arguments used by the church to try to make people wait until they were married before having full sexual intercourse would have lacked any credibility in the eyes of the young people. For example, 'Your body is a temple of the Holy Spirit. Flee from sexual immorality' (1 Corinthians 6.18–19). This was an argument written for Christians. It was an argument that meant nothing to the young people, who had no concept of their bodies as 'temples of the Holy Spirit'. If we tried to tell them that they should not have sexual intercourse until they were married, because they were temples of the Holy Spirit, they would simply think of us as 'divs' (fools).

In the eyes of the young people, the figure of Jesus was hedged round with a barbed wire fence of morality. As Christians, we are taught that our immorality can come between us and Christ; we are not taught that our morality can come between other people and Christ. The young people saw Christians as people who did not do things. They were people who did not have sex; they were people who did not take drugs. How did we get over this hurdle?

We wanted to make connections between the young people and God. If we laid down the law over sex, not only were we not going to make any connections but we were also not going to teach them anything about Christ. We might teach them about ethics or morality or respectable behaviour but we would not teach them about Jesus.

What we did was to get the young people to think for themselves about sex in a logical way. Sex became a logical issue to the young women when we worked with them on how they might respond when their partner wanted to have sex with them. We said to them, 'Say no if you don't want to have sex. Have some self-respect. Raise your standards. Don't settle for anything that is second best.' Self-respect was a big issue. The expectations of the young people were not high.

'I bet I marry someone who beats me up!' said Michelle, one of the young people. We were walking along the street towards the church, and Michelle's comment was delivered with no more emotion than she might have used talking about going shopping or doing some schoolwork. She looked upon the idea of marrying someone who beat her up as an accepted part of life because that was all she had ever seen.

We knew that the kids were sleeping with each other and whatever we said was not going to keep them out of each other's beds. Therefore we needed to talk through the realities of having sex. We would say, 'If you are going to have sex then think of the consequences.'

There are good reasons for not having sex before you are married and in order to put across these reasons we acted out a sketch at our evening service. We were demonstrating the logic of God: we have been given our body as something beautiful that should not be thrown away on one drunken night or on an evening when we felt vulnerable. We wanted to say that sex was beautiful in a loving relationship and that was what God wanted us to have. He does not want us to feel dirty or guilty about sex. The sketch that we did was short and simply done with a minimum of rehearsal. In the first scene the boy was pressurizing the girl to have sex with him.

'I love you. Don't you love me? If you loved me then you would sleep with me. You obviously don't love me.'

'You know that I love you. Why do I have to sleep
with you to prove it? Can't I just iron you a shirt?'
'You either sleep with me to prove that you love me
or I'm off.'

In the second scene they were having sex. In the third
scene she went to see him.

'I'm pregnant. What am I going to do?'
'Is it mine?'
'What?!'
'How do I know that it is mine?'

She ends up in tears. He is not interested in her any
more. He was the hunter and he has caught his prey and
now he is looking for new game. The young people
watched the play with rapt attention and after it finished,
they sat in silence. 'I wish you had done that play a week
ago' was what one young woman said. This comment
chilled us. It made us realize how urgent our work was.
She has now got a baby and her boyfriend has left her.

What we were trying to do was to make the young
people see sex as a logical issue rather than a moral
issue. There is a logic behind a refusal to be pressur-
ized into having sex with your partner. This logic is
especially relevant to the women who have more to lose
than the men. The man that sleeps around is known as
a stud. The woman that sleeps around is known as a
slag. There is a logic behind refusing to have sex
outside a loving relationship. We were not doing a
marriage preparation course teaching Christians about
the biblical view of marriage. We were working with
young people and condensing the Christian truth into
thoughts that were logical to their idiom.

What we told them was that being tempted to have
sex and then resisting that temptation is a test of true
character. If the girl in the sketch had resisted the boy,
then whatever the outcome he would have had more
respect for her.

'If you are tempted by something, you want it badly; if you resist that temptation, the reason you resist is that you have come to the conclusion that it is wrong to give in. It is not the sex that is wrong; it is not even the temptation that is wrong. It is the giving in to the temptation that is wrong. If you give into temptation one evening because you are drunk you are letting yourself down. You wake up in the morning feeling cheap and dirty. If you say "no" to sex you can feel proud of yourself.'

We also told them that Jesus was tempted. He knew that he was going to die and knew why he was going to die, yet he still asked God if he could be let off. Jesus did not want to go through with the crucifixion. He wanted an easier way out. There is nothing easy about resisting temptation but resisting his temptation made Jesus who he was.

In telling the young people about Jesus we were uncovering the effects of years of negativity and low self-esteem. They went to schools where little was expected of them and they were used to people putting them down. We wanted the young people to know that we loved them and we wanted this to give them confidence to make decisions for themselves. What was the right thing for the girl in the sketch to have done? We told them to work through the logic of the situation and live by their answer.

On another occasion Eddie was talking with Ricky. Ricky was one of the club members at CUM – good-looking, very sensible and with a lot of girls falling at his feet. Ricky asked,

'Why is it wrong to have sex?'
'It isn't wrong', Eddie replied.
'What do you mean?' said Ricky. 'I thought the Bible said that it was wrong to have sex outside marriage.'
'Put it this way', said Eddie. 'If you were going to get married would you rather marry a virgin or some

scrubber that has been out with everyone in the street?'

'I would rather marry the virgin', Ricky replied.

'Exactly', said Eddie. 'That is what the Bible teaches.'

'Yes', said Ricky. 'That makes a lot of sense.'

We were not dealing with sex in a school curriculum manner. In theory Ricky might have gone away from the conversation thinking that he could have more fun with the 'scrubber' in the meantime. In theory, he might have gone away from the conversation thinking that it was all right for him to sleep around but not for a woman to do so. In practice he did not; he knew Eddie and in the context of their relationship he knew exactly what Eddie was saying. What Eddie was doing was posing questions about sex and then challenging him to work out the 'rights' and the 'wrongs' for himself. Paul highlights the role of conscience and discretion in understanding what God might want from a situation.

> Though I am free and belong to no man, I make myself a slave to everyone, to win as many as possible. To the Jews I became like a Jew, to win the Jews. To those under the law I became like one under the law (though I myself am not under the law), so as to win those under the law. To those not having the law I became like one not having the law. To the weak I became weak, to win the weak. I have become all things to all men so that by all possible means I might save some (1 Corinthians 9.19-22).

This passage became a marching cry for the work that we did.

We hurled a barrage of thoughts at the young people to challenge them to think differently about sex. We did not say to them: 'Sleeping with your partner is wrong.' We talked with them about the possible consequences ... slander – 'she is a slag'; a baby at seventeen;

parents angry; your whole life turned upside down.

We talked about how God wants for us the most beautiful things that we can imagine. We talked about how we cannot imagine the beauty of what God wants for us. God gives us sex as a beautiful thing but he also gives us choice.

'You are doing yourself out of a beautiful relationship. The first prize is the untouched love affair – two people knowing only each other; the second prize is mediocrity ... If you are working and you save your wages and you buy a jersey for £150, are you going to treat it better than a cheap acrylic jersey that you find dumped by someone?'

It was a reasonable question and it was putting things on a level that the young people could think on and work out for themselves.

By making sex a logical issue to the young people we were not suggesting that it ceased to be a moral issue when tackled outside the framework of the church. Any idea that there was one rule for believing Christians and another for non-believing young people is an ethical apartheid. The reason that we appealed to the young people's logic was because it was their logic that would lead them to Jesus. There was plenty of time for them to understand more fully the teachings about sex once they got to know Jesus. We knew that the teachings of Jesus could only be fully understood in the context of knowing him.

5
Drugs

As touching to please God, there is no work better than
another ... whether thou be an apostle or a shoe maker ...
Thou art a kitchen page and washest thy master's dishes,
another is an apostle and preacheth the word of God ...
Now if thou comparest deed to deed there is difference
betwixt washing of dishes and preaching of the word of
God. But as to please God none at all.

(William Tyndale)

Some of the young people would smoke a joint before
coming into the service and they would go outside and
smoke during the service. We were not dealing with
heroin addicts or cocaine addicts. We did not want to
condone the cannabis but we did not want the fact that
someone was smoking cannabis to be a barrier to him
getting to know God. We did not want to make giving
up cannabis a precondition of them hearing the
gospel. The whole point of Christ's death is that there
are no preconditions and that he died for us while we
were yet sinners (Romans 5.8). Cannabis was not a
salvation issue and who were we to deny God's power
and make a prejudgement that he could not work
through a cannabis buzz?

We did not have to spell out to the young people that
smoking cannabis was a big deal because they already
knew. If they had not been arrested themselves for
possession they all knew of someone who had. We were
not going to rush into condemning the young people

because there were plenty of people doing that already and our condemnation might be the barrier to them getting to know God.

The fact that we did not make an issue over drugs gave us an opportunity to talk about Christ. If we had told the young people that they could not smoke or drink when they came into church then they would not have come at all. If we had told them that the Bible says you should not take drugs, then their interest in the Bible would have fallen at the first hurdle and then they would not get to know Jesus.

Eddie was involved in a drug culture before he became a Christian. Now that he is a Christian he has been taught to put this part of his life behind him. However, if putting this part of his life behind him means being ashamed for what he has done then the effect is self-defeating since this was the one area that was crucial to the work in connecting with the young people, understanding them and relating Jesus to them. The experience of being involved with drugs provided a common denominator with the young people.

Being forgiven by Jesus means that Eddie can rejoice in the life that he lived before he became a Christian. Any hint that he should be ashamed of what he did before he knew Jesus is spineless because it is not trusting in God's plan for his life. Every breath that he took before he became a Christian was vital in relating to the pre-non Christian young people.

William Tyndale was put to death for heresy because he translated the Bible into a language that everyone could understand. He did not believe that people should have to understand Latin in order to read Jesus' teaching. What we were saying five hundred years later was that the young people should not have to jump through the hoops of always having to understand other people's interpretations of the Bible in order to have the chance of working out what the text meant for themselves and for their own daily lives.

We gave Bibles to the young people to read and they saw it as being full of people on trips induced by God. What about Peter seeing a sheet with animals floating down from heaven? What about Isaiah when he saw a vision in the temple? What about the book of Revelation? We wanted to take the Bible for what it was and not put safe, socially conditioned interpretations on to everything that we read. Through being with Eddie and the young people I realized that in order to identify with them I had to try to tune in to their way of thinking, and rather than rushing to condemn them as wrong Eddie and I gave them space so that they could work things through for themselves.

We allowed some of the imagery and language associated with drugs to explain ideas about Christianity to the kids. We were putting our theology into a context they understood. We used to sing 'Marching in the kingdom of God' with everyone stamping on the pews and shouting at the tops of their voices. We would then let the young people change the wording to draw in ideas that they could relate to. We would sing 'tripping in the kingdom of God' followed by 'buzzing (good feelings) in the kingdom of God' followed by 'snogging in the kingdom of God'.

We were using the imagery that the young people understood in order to explain to them the things of God and to make them feel comfortable within the confines of the church. It opened things up. It took away the ideas of rules and regulations that were putting them off getting to know Jesus. They laughed. They tried to think of words that would shock us and that they would not be 'allowed' to say. However, as fast as they thought of an idea then we would add another verse in order to include it in what we were singing.

We were using imagery that the young people understood as a way for them to learn about Jesus. If they asked questions, we would explain to them what we were singing. For example, when we sang about 'snogging in the kingdom of God' we were referring to people either in a loving relationship or else married. If you were 'rumping in the kingdom of God' it meant that you would be married; sexual intercourse in the kingdom of God meant marriage. When we sang 'tripping in the kingdom of God' we were referring to a time when God might give someone a vision. When we sang 'buzzing in the kingdom of God' we were referring to good feelings, being full of the Spirit, full of joy, certainty, peace.

I thought that we were being radical when we used the imagery of drugs and sex to explain what it was like knowing Jesus. The fact that I felt this illustrates how insular had been all that I had been taught about how to present Christianity to non-believers. Paul gives one presentation of Christianity to Jews and God-fearing Gentiles in Antioch (Acts 13.16-41), but gives a completely different presentation to the Greeks at Athens (Acts 17.22-31). The beginning of John's Gospel uses imagery from Greek philosophy to explain Christianity. We were using imagery from Bermondsey philosophy to tell the young people about Jesus. This thinking is second nature to African and Indian theologians who know that every time you approach a different tribe you have to learn their customs before you can speak to them about Jesus. The young people were like a tribe with their own language and customs, and our job was to root our presentation of Jesus in ideas that they understood.

6

Rock and Roll

Let God's word try every man's doctrine and whomsoever God's word proveth unclean let him be taken for a leper. One Scripture will help to declare another. And the circumstances, that is to say, the places that go before and after, will give light unto the middle text. And the open and manifest Scriptures will ever improve the false and wrong exposition of the darker sentences.

(William Tyndale)

Eddie is an actor and a musician. He had got his Equity card through doing gigs in pubs. His vision was that what he had done in pubs could be transferred into a church context and through doing this we could set up a worship service for the young people.

There was to be a group of us, who sang at the front of the church. The thinking was that the young people were free to join in with the singing or not, as they wanted. It would be like a pub with a band playing. Anyone in the pub could ignore the music or listen to the music or sing along with it. The young people were free to sit and talk, kneel, sit down, stand up, jump all over the pews, do whatever they wanted.

We believed that if a core group of people were singing and worshipping, the young people would get drawn into what was going on. Having the service in the church was an integral part of Eddie's vision. Churches are seen by young people as places that are either locked or else they are just places for old people.

We wanted to smash the idea that churches were a no-go area for young people and enable them to see church as something relevant and accessible.

The vision was not for Bible studies with rows of teenagers having the Gospels explained to them; the vision was for worship with young people singing songs to God. What did it matter whether or not they understood what they were singing? We saw worshipping God as an instinct and the most natural thing in the world and they had as much right to worship God as anyone else. We did not want the differences between a church culture and a young person's culture to remain a barrier. We wanted the idea of young people coming into church to be as natural to them as the idea of going into a pub.

It seemed a simple idea but it was difficult to put into practice. The first difficulty was that we only knew one way to conduct a worship service and that was to conduct a service for believing Christians. We had no experience of doing anything else. We found that we got dragged into a system of worship appropriate only for Christians in that everyone agreed with what we were saying and loved what we were doing. They were special meaningful times and we felt blessed by God – great; lucky us! On one occasion we even taped the sound of our songs and played them back at frequent intervals during the week, feeling that we had struck on something special.

However, it was not the vision that we were seeking to realize. The trouble was that we were giving food to people who had already had a square meal and we were ignoring the people who were hungry. We knew that God wanted us to work with the young people but we did not know how. The young people were nowhere to be seen. We knew that we had to be at church each Sunday evening but we did not have a clue what was going to happen. The more special and meaningful the Sunday evenings were to the Christians, the more frustrated we became because it was not the work that God had given us to do.

When we prayed we both got angry and even more frustrated – 'Come on, God, what is happening?' There was one Sunday when I lay in bed all day, feeling dreadful. I had a temperature of a hundred and four and had told Eddie that I would not come to the service. Come the evening I felt that I had something that needed to be said. I sat in the church and shivered my way through the songs that Eddie sang and then I stood up and said that however long it took we would keep worshipping until young people appeared. I talked about Moses. The only preparation that I had for what I was saying was a horror at the idea of him spending forty years in the wilderness and then not being allowed into the promised land. There was one occasion when he had despaired and struck the rock so that water came out of it (Numbers 20.7-13). It was because of this that God, a terribly hard taskmaster, did not allow him to enter the promised land. I said that this story was like us doing the service for forty years; despairing of anything ever happening in year thirty-seven and finally as we hobble out of the door as old men, we would look over our shoulders and see young people filling the church up.

I went home as soon as I had spoken and went to bed. At two o'clock in the morning I was admitted to hospital and diagnosed as suffering from colitis. I had gone in a few short hours from preaching the word of God to being unable to control even my bowel movements. The hard lesson that I had to learn and that I had to go to hospital to understand fully was that we wanted things done in our own time and that we had to wait for God to do things in his own time.

The situation changed when Eddie went up to the group of young people, who were smoking joints and drinking beer, hanging around outside the church, and asked them if they would like to come in for the service. No one had ever asked them to come into a church before and they were curious about what we were doing and why he had invited them inside.

When the young people came into the church, they shouted, swore, ran around, and slouched in the corner drinking beers. They went into the organ loft, chucked coffee round the vestry, smoked and shouted out to each other. In a stroke we destroyed the framework of the worship service that had been developing. Christians, who had been coming for one thing, to their consternation were confronted with something completely different. People felt confused and frightened. They had been blessed by what we had been doing and they could not understand why we would allow the young people to destroy what had been created.

It was very painful to destroy something that we had put a lot of time and energy into creating. However, doing so was a part of the natural progression of reaching the young people. We needed to destroy what we had created in order to break new ground. We could have spent the next twenty years running a service that built up people who already knew and believed in Jesus. However, none of this would have helped us reach pre-non Christian young people and that, we knew, was our mission from God. We were creating something that was so alien to the concept of a structured and safe worship service that people could really not understand what was happening.

Some thought that what had happened was of the devil, and when we disagreed they accused us of arrogance. One woman, who had come from a different church, wrote us a letter explaining why she could not agree with what had happened and telling us how she could not be involved in the service any longer. We were standing the idea of 'going to church to receive' on its head. Work with pre-non Christians was uncomfortable and difficult for me. For the Christians it was hard work, and they could end the service feeling tired and maybe worse than they had at the beginning.

We were creating an environment that pre-non Christian young people could feel at home in. Each Sunday was a jumble of different events. On one occasion Eddie was at the front of the church playing his guitar and I stood looking at Alan, one of the young people, standing at the back of the church, his long blond hair tied tightly back in a pony tail, his pale thin face sneering at the frenzied activity in the service going on around him. People were standing at the front of the church, shouting out the words of the song that Eddie was playing.

'All right, Alan.'
'All right, Bob.'

He was wearing a frayed leather jacket, older but better quality than my recently purchased high-street chain-store suede leather jacket.

'Swap', I said.
'You what?'
'Swap – you take my jacket and I'll take yours. Your jacket is better quality but mine is a lot newer so go on, swap.'

He smiled and we swapped jackets. It was a spontaneous gesture, not expected by Alan, that marked the service for him. I know this as two years later he reminded me of the incident in a letter he sent me from prison.

We were creating a cocktail of chaos. We were taking the raw sin of young people from off the street and were bringing it into direct contact with the Holy Spirit of God. We were making up a mixture of high explosives. Naïve, blind, pigheaded and determined? Of course we were, but if we had not been, we would never have done anything. Sunday evenings would never have got beyond *Songs of Praise* or whatever film was on television and the kids would never have heard about Jesus.

7

Unchurching the Churched

> It was not for naught that Christ bade beware of the leaven of the Pharisees. Nothing is so sweet that they make not sour with their traditions. The evangelion, that joyful tidings, is now bitterer than the old law, Christ's burden is heavier than the yoke of Moses, our condition and estate is ten times more grievous than ever was the Jews'.
>
> *(William Tyndale)*

We had to work in two different cultures. One culture was created by the young people and it focused on the park area surrounding the church, where they used to hang around. The other culture was created by the Christians and it focused on the church building. The culture of the young people was active, spontaneous, unthought-out and instinctive. The culture of the church was passive, thought-through, programmed and planned. I needed to learn not to be defensive about the church culture but be prepared to learn from the young people's culture.

The church culture of Sunday mornings – singing hymns, listening to sermons and joining in prayers – was designed to teach Christians about God. It was not designed to teach pre-non Christians about God, nor was it designed to teach Christians about how to share their faith with pre-non Christians. The language used about God in church assumed a knowledge base and a level of commitment that was not present in the pre-non Christian young person. The result was that there was one language about God used in the church and another language which we used with the young people. We needed to break down the assumption that we could talk about God to the young people in the same way that we might talk about God in a church context. This involved deprogramming myself and other Christians – 'unchurching the churched' – in order to enable us to share our faith with pre-non Christian young people.

The language used about God in church is deductive. The dictionary definition of 'deduction' is 'the inference of a particular truth from a general truth previously known'. The church takes the Bible as the general truth and draws particular truths out of it. For example, your body is a temple of the Holy Spirit (general truth) – therefore you should not smoke (particular truth).

This approach is beautiful and understandable. It is an acceptable process when you know something about God; this process is only relevant, however, when people do know something about God and accept the general premise that the Bible is authoritative. The church presents its deductive conclusions because it is catering for people who know Christ and therefore want to know the teaching from the Bible. If people do not know Christ, any deductive conclusions, such as 'do not have sex outside marriage', are not relevant to them because they do not have the background context of knowing Jesus and the initial premise of the Bible as authoritative.

Induction is the opposite to deduction. The dictionary definition of 'induction' is 'the reasoning from particular truths to general truths'. Inductive teaching happens when you encourage the other person to work things out for themselves and come to their own conclusions. Inductive thinking starts with the specific situation and works outwards from that situation to come to a conclusion. For example, the church says that sex outside marriage is wrong. The inductive thinker works it out for herself on the basis of thoughts, feelings and experiences. She takes the teaching, chews it about, thinks about it, decides that she cannot understand it, does what the teaching condemns and then, through doing this, realizes what it was all about and finally decides whether she thinks it was right or wrong.

This approach is representative of that used by a pre-non Christian. The young people were naturally inductive thinkers. If they wanted to do something they would do it and then face the consequences. They were not going to listen to deductive presentations about Christ's teaching because they had no knowledge of Christ. Telling them that Christ's teaching should be obeyed killed the teaching as good news and made them view the teaching with the label of authority – and they had no respect for authority. We needed to develop teaching methods that enabled the young people to work Jesus out for themselves and build an independent relationship with God.

However hard we might work at making deductive thinking more and more accessible and more and more simple, to the young people, who were inductive doers, it would still mean nothing. We needed to meet them with an inductive approach. We described Christ's teaching in a way that enabled them to work it through for themselves rather than prescribing Christian behaviour in a way that laid down the law. What we were saying to the young people was: 'Think things through and work things out for yourself.' What the young people heard the church saying was: 'Obey Christ's teachings!' As the young people did not know Christ, what he might or might not have said was irrelevant, and being told to obey what he said was a 'liberty' (unforgivable action).

Eddie did an 'inductive' gospel presentation. He read a passage from *Winnie-the-Pooh*, and then read a different passage about the police fitting a man up (fabricating evidence), throwing him in prison and then sentencing him to the electric chair.

'To you, which of the two passages is real?' he asked.
'The geezer who was fitted up by the police', the young people replied.
'Where do you think that it came from?'
'A newspaper.'
'No, the Bible – Jesus being arrested and having lies told about him.'

This was an inductive approach to teaching the Bible because rather than telling the young people that the word of God was true – 'This is the story. Now believe it' – Eddie gave them the opportunity to decide whether the story sounded real and believable and then to decide whether they believed Jesus' story.

On another occasion, Eddie held up his hand and asked 'Who believes that I have got a £1 coin in my hand? I will give it to the first person who comes up and asks for it.' Initially the young people were hesitant, fearing a trick, but as soon as someone committed himself to ask for it then he was given the £1 coin. Eddie then said 'You believed me and you were given the £1. It's as easy as that with God – if you choose to believe him he has good things to give you.'

This inductive approach to teaching put the responsibility on to the young people to work things out for themselves rather than requiring them to accept what they were being told without questioning it.

At an epilogue in CUM Eddie got all of the young people to follow him round the room. He did not say why he wanted them to do this but after they had followed him for a few minutes he stopped and told them that what they had done with him was the same in origin as what the disciples had done with Jesus when they agreed to follow him. This approach to teaching broke down the ideas of Christianity into portions that the young people could chew on for themselves. When the disciples of John the Baptist went to Jesus and asked whether he was the one who was to come or whether they should wait for another, Jesus told them to look around and to work it out for themselves (Matthew 11.5).

The inheritance that I had from twenty years of going to church was a deadened ability to work things out for myself. I thought I should be obedient to the Bible and do what I was told in church. I needed to shake off a legacy of inertia so that I could understand Jesus for myself and teach about Jesus to the young people. When I was taught about Christianity, I was taught to rely on authority. Eddie, however, was taught about Christianity through his relationship with God. He relied on God to convict him of what was right and what was wrong. He learnt instinctively and impulsively and that is the direction we took with the young people. Knowing God could be as natural as Adam and Eve walking in the Garden of Eden or as immediate as Jesus praying to his father.

In order to work with the young people, I needed to train myself to trust my instincts and impulses rather than wait for some hidden hand of authority to tell me that what I wanted to do was alright.

I was looking for a place to park my car. The whole of one side of a street was clear. People obviously thought that because no one was parking there, it must mean that no one was allowed to park there. Working it out for myself, I parked the car and by the time I got out every single other space in the street was full. On each of those two occasions I had trusted to my instincts and if I had made a mistake, I would have apologized and either moved my car or eaten my picnic elsewhere.

Trusting our own instincts means that we have to trust God to guide us and believe that if we do something wrong, he will let us know. If we trust God to guide us when we make mistakes, we are thinking inductively and relying on God, instinct and common sense to work things out.

It took a non-believer to reaffirm this to me. I was having tea with him in the Grand Hotel in Brighton. He finished his tea. He had eaten all that he wanted. Working things out for himself, he pulled out a cigarette and started to smoke.

'Can I have an ashtray?' he asked.

'I'm afraid that you're not allowed to smoke', he was told by a waitress.

'I am sorry', he said. 'I had not realized. However, now that I've started my cigarette, could you bring me an ashtray so that I can finish it?'

She brought him an ashtray and he finished his cigarette. He looked at me and smiled. I raised my eyebrows in question. He said, 'It is always easier to ask for forgiveness than to seek permission.'

The inductive teaching that Eddie and I developed with the young people was about instinct and impulse. It was about 'asking for forgiveness' rather than 'seeking permission'. It was about learning from their mistakes and working things out for themselves.

'Doing what we are told' is more to do with 'seeking permission' than 'asking for forgiveness'. If we are made to feel that we have to 'seek permission' before we take a decision then we begin to feel that it is wrong to make a mistake. However, Jesus is all about 'asking for forgiveness' when we make a mistake. If none of us ever makes any mistakes, what was the point of Jesus' death? He died so that we could learn from our mistakes and not feel guilty about them. If we feel guilty about our mistakes, we obviously do not understand forgiveness and our mistakes become a barrier to knowing God. If we learn from our mistakes, then they become an opportunity to draw closer to God.

Once I had realized this I began to see illustrations all over the place. I play rugby each week for a pub team in north London. I made a mistake one week when we were losing in an important league match. One of the opposition pulled me out of the scrum, threw me to the ground, jumped on top of me and started to head-butt me. Players from both sides piled in to pull us apart. I was very angry with him and lost control of myself. I ran at him and decked him one with a neat right-hander.

The church only says one thing to that situation: 'Don't do it; don't make mistakes.' I knew that. I realized, after I had hit him, that I was wrong in what I had done. 'Don't get angry'. Great! However, if someone has you pinned to the ground and is smashing their head against your nose, it is hard not to get angry. I knew that I was wrong to get angry so 'don't get angry' was no good to me. It would have been like saying to an ill person 'don't get ill'.

Jesus taught about how mistakes could bring people closer to God. He told the story of the Pharisee and the publican, who went into the temple to pray. It was the publican who had made the bigger mistakes and it was the publican who was closer to God. In Jesus' story of the two men owing money, it was the one who had well and truly messed up his life and ended up owing five hundred denarii (as opposed to the fifty denarii that the other one owed) who ended up better off than the one who only owed a tenth of that amount. That is the nature of forgiveness – you learn from your mistakes.

Things that are this simple can often be more powerful. John Lennon spent the latter part of the sixties fuelling his organic need for art. He was a musician but his true vocation was art. He found himself getting drawn into art exhibitions. He knew that he was looking for something but he was not sure what. He walked into an exhibition and he spotted a stepladder. Above the stepladder hanging from the ceiling was a magnifying glass. Above the magnifying glass was a dot on the ceiling. He climbed to the top of the ladder and looked at the dot through the magnifying glass. He saw the word 'Yes'. The positiveness of the greeting sold the exhibition to him. The artist was Yoko Ono.

Christianity is just as basic and simple – Jesus died to forgive us our sins and the logic of this forgiveness is that we can learn from our mistakes. Knowing that we are forgiven by God is more important than worrying about whether we are 'right' or 'wrong' in the decisions we take. If we do not know the reality of Christ's forgiveness we cannot teach it.

Eddie understands more about forgiveness than anyone else that I have ever met. He understands forgiveness because he understands about judgement. He understands about judgement because he had been judged and condemned on a previous occasion by society and spent fifteen months in prison for possession of cannabis. He had done something wrong and he knew it and accepted that he was guilty. It was this that enabled him to understand how incredible it was to be forgiven.

When we taught the young people that a real way to God was through our mistakes then it made Jesus more real and accessible to them. I wish that I had worked this out when I met Pete in Luton, when I was still working there as a curate. I was leading a course for people to learn about Christianity. Pete and I met up soon after he had been released from prison. It was early summer and we used to sit in the garden with the evenings lengthening and talk about Christianity. He came along to the course.

He fancied Jackie, one of the women on the course. He asked me what I thought he should do. He did not want to go out with her but he did want some sex and she seemed willing. I pleaded with him not to sleep with her, telling him that sleeping with her would feel good in the short term but not in the long term. I told him that what he was learning about Christianity would help him for the rest of his life. 'So, don't chuck away your big chance to learn about Christianity', I told him.

Things came to a head on the sixth week of the course, which was held in the church. All the people who had been coming to the course were invited to respond to what they had heard. I talked with Pete and asked him if he wanted to become a Christian. His face was a study of concentration. I pleaded with him. 'Look, Pete, you're a hard lad and you're not frightened of anyone on the estate, right?' He nodded. 'So why are you so frightened of committing your life to God and becoming a Christian?'

He dropped his eyes, his shoulders slumped and he could no longer hold my gaze. At that moment Jackie got up and walked out of the church. He stood up and followed her. Six hours later, at three o'clock in the morning, I was woken up by Pete. He had come straight from Jackie's bed, feeling guilty at what he had done. He wanted me to tell him that everything was all right. I did not handle the situation well. I felt that he had a responsibility to Jackie and told him that he had made his choice and that he should go back to bed with Jackie, who was waiting for him. It felt to me like 'yes' and 'no', 'right' and 'wrong', 'black' and 'white'.

It felt to me as if Pete was given a choice earlier on in the evening and because he did not make the choice there and then, he had somehow lost the opportunity. What I said to him was both restrictive and inadequate. In telling him to go back to bed with Jackie, I felt that I was sending the sinner away into the night, as if I was saying that he had had his opportunity to learn about God and he had blown it. Sorry, Pete, I was still learning. If I had known then what I know now, I might still have suggested that you went back to Jackie for the rest of the night, but I would have invited you over for breakfast the next morning to talk about God.

8
Faith and Prayer

> And in the Universities they have ordained that no man shall look in the Scriptures until he be noselled (nursed) in heathen learning eight or nine years and armed with false principles with which he is clean shut out of the understanding of Scripture.
>
> *(William Tyndale)*

When Eddie and I prayed with the young people, we were encouraging them to build up their experience and then to form an understanding of prayer out of that experience. When Eddie and I prayed with each other we were building the foundations for everything that happened with the young people. 'How do you pray?' the young people would say. 'I have never prayed before. What do you do?'

I would tell them to start by talking to the ceiling and then work upwards towards God. It was not a developed concept of prayer but that was not the point. The point was that they were working prayer out for themselves. If we tried to explain the concept of prayer we would have complicated a basic instinct. Someone on a boat that is sinking might still cry out for help even if he thinks there is no one to hear him.

One of the young people said, 'It's embarrassing to pray when your mates are around.' What Eddie said was, 'When you are alone in bed at night, try it ... give it a go ... if you have got something to ask for, then ask for it ... see what happens ... you have got nothing to lose ... why not?'

Kirk prayed that he would not get sent to prison and walked out of court a free man. Ricky prayed for a job and got one. Ricky used to meet with Eddie in his flat to talk through the Bible. He said to Eddie,

'I've been praying to God and he hasn't answered my prayers.'
'What have you been asking for?' said Eddie, thinking that Ricky had probably been asking for something along the lines of a Porsche or a million pounds.
'I've been praying for a job.'
'What jobs have you been up for?'
'I've been up for three jobs – bricklayer, plumber and electrician.'
'Do you have any more interviews?'
'No, but I've applied for a job as a heating engineer.'
'Come on then, we'll ask God to give it to you.'

Eddie prayed aloud with Ricky. In his head he was saying,

'God, we are trying so hard down here – give Ricky this job. You have called me to do this work; you have got to give me something. If you want these kids to be Christians, you have got to start proving yourself to them. If you don't do this, then there is half a chance of losing me as well.'

The prayer meant as much to him as it did to Ricky, because if nothing happened and Ricky did not get an interview, Eddie was going to feel angry and disillusioned with God.

Four days later, Eddie saw Ricky and asked if he had heard about the interview. Ricky said, 'I start the job next Monday – not just as a heating engineer but one better than that. They want me as a supervisor.' Ricky was off on a four-year apprenticeship. The incident blew both their minds.

What Eddie was teaching Ricky was that you abuse people by asking for too much; you abuse God by asking for too little. Eddie and I would always ask when we prayed. We did not know if we were going to get what we asked for, but it seemed crazy not to ask. We did a sketch on this, looking at which was the better approach. In it Eddie came up to me:

'Hello, Bob, lovely trousers you've got on; they look really great. What you did last week was fantastic. You're such a lovely geezer, er, um, could you possibly, please, if you don't mind that is, lend me a tenner?'

I gave him the tenner grudgingly because he had insulted our friendship by trying to butter me up and not asking outright for the money. Then Eddie came up to me and said,

'Hello, Bob, can I borrow a tenner?'
'Yeah, sure.'

If Eddie wanted to borrow a tenner, I would have lent him the money because he was my friend. If he thought that he had to compliment me and put me on a pedestal in order to persuade me to lend the money then he would have been insulting our friendship. We told the young people that it was the same with God. 'If you want something, just ask. You might not get what you want, but ask. Don't beat about the bush but be straight and up front with God in what you want.'

Eddie and I prayed together each week for two years. It was soon after we started to pray together that I developed colitis. Colitis was like a messenger from God teaching me to pray and to have faith – but colitis drove me beyond faith to sheer desperation. On one occasion I was standing in the middle of a supermarket and did not have a chance even to think about reaching a toilet before it was too late. I was crying with humiliation. The same thing happened when I took a ten-minute drive to go to a meeting at the Southwark Youth Office. Each week, when we met, we prayed that

I would be healed from the colitis. We prayed for healing, sweating, lying on the floor and pleading with God. If God was not going to heal me, then it seemed as if I would have to stop work and resign from my position as director of CUM. I realized that God had answered our prayers and that I was healed as I started to go to the toilet less and less frequently. The healing was a miracle from God but it was not done in isolation. It also needed me to change my lifestyle. I had to eat more sensibly and live more carefully – less stress, more vegetables and fruit and earlier nights.

We prayed front-line prayers for the work with the young people. Meeting to pray was often the only preparation that we had for the Sunday services. 'Father help us ... show us what to do ... forgive us our anger ... protect us.'

When he prayed, Eddie's use of tenses mirrored the prophets in the Old Testament. The prophets would use a past tense in a future setting. Rather than saying that something will happen, they would say that something had happened as a reflection of their faith in God. Eddie would talk and pray about the coming Sunday in this vein, as if it had already happened – 'Don't worry, it is done. Sorted!' It was confidence in ourselves through having confidence in God.

As we were working with pre-non Christians we could not teach them any theoretical or conceptual understandings of God. What we taught had to be real and immediate. If I tried to teach prayer as a conceptual thing, I would not get very far. The young people had heard people praying and thought it sounded stupid. The language meant nothing to them and it did not sound like a real conversation. We taught them that prayer was about being real before God – 'Hello, God, how are you doing?'

They could understand this conversational approach to praying and thus we were removing blocks and drawing them closer into an understanding of God.

We were armed only with faith in God and a blind trust. We would turn up at the church with nothing planned, plug in the guitar and start. The times that we did have something planned, we always seemed to end up doing something different.

When we prayed, we would meet together on the Wednesday to pray for the coming Sunday and to ask God for his guidance and freedom. We would talk, shout, sit, kneel, lie on the floor or walk around. We could be angry, distracted or upset. When we prayed, we were not asking, we were demanding things of God. God was educating us about prayer. Whatever situations were hurled at us, we flung them back at God.

9
Black and White, Working Class and Middle Class

> The king ought to count what he hath spent in the Pope's quarrel since he was king ... I do not doubt but that it will surmount the sum of forty or fifty hundred thousand pounds. The king therefore ought to make them pay this money every farthing and fetch it out of their mitres, crosses, shrines and all manner treasure of the church, and pay it to his commons again.
>
> *(William Tyndale)*

Any system of power survives by incorporating rather than opposing anything that is too threatening – the hymn 'Jerusalem' was originally written as something satirical and anti-establishment: '... did those feet ... walk ... in England's green and pleasant land?' The original hymn was a howl of protest at the industrialization of the countryside. Now it has become the marching song of the establishment and is sung at public schools as an expression of being English and proud.

Charles Dickens was a soldier of socialism and wrote revolutionary tracts which were serialized in magazines, highlighting the dreadful poverty that existed in London. The stories were powerful enough in themselves to have stood the test of time. As a result they have been trivialized and sentimentalized out of existence. Lionel Bart converted *Oliver Twist* into a musical with brightly-scrubbed, cherubic-faced chimney-sweeps dancing and singing across the streets of London. The establishment survives by taking things that are too threatening and incorporating them into their own structure, thereby disarming them.

There are two mistakes that people may make when they read a Christian book. One mistake is to assume that the person writing the book is an expert and that the reader should use the book as a handbook and copy them. The other mistake is to assume that the person writing the book is a hero and that the reader should admire them – good old Eddie and Bob working with the kids in the inner city. Both of these two responses assimilate what is being said into the ongoing work of the church and so turn it into a success story, rather than recognizing that what is being said is a challenge.

We worked with the young people despite, and not because of, the training and nurture that we received through the church at large. A 'Catch 22' situation emerged. We were working with pre-non Christian young people in the inner city; people heard about what we were doing and felt that there was no need for them to do anything because someone else was doing it.

The issue is exactly the same with regard to how the Church of England, shot through with middle-class standards, values and behaviour, relates to a working-class culture. The Church of England incorporates working-class people into a middle-class system and then holds them up as examples of success in order to support that system – as proof that a middle-class church can relate to working-class people.

There is no middle class and no working class in Christ. Eddie jumped over a fence to avoid taking school exams. I took my exams twice because I wanted to go to university. So what? We were one in Christ. Our two environments could not have been more extreme and different. I grew up in Wimbledon in a lovely big house.

Eddie grew up in Bermondsey in a council block. I grew up with six people in a ten-bedroomed house; Eddie grew up with six people in a three-bedroomed flat. When we were actually working together with the young people, class differences were not an issue because we were concentrating on what we had in common: our belief in God and our commitment to his work.

When we thought about how we worked together, however, and when we analysed our methods of relating God to the young people, we realized that we were both coming to the work from very different perspectives. The fact of our different upbringings and backgrounds was not an issue between the two of us but it was, and is, a very big issue in terms of relating Christ to the young people. I was a 'middle-class' vicar full of church 'do's' and 'don't s' and was full of the textbook answers to the usual questions on the Trinity, the theology of salvation or whatever people expected to hear in church on a Sunday morning. Eddie had been a 'working-class' Christian for only five months and, before becoming a Christian, had had little knowledge of God other than what he had experienced and found out for himself from the Bible. The Church system and its hierarchy meant nothing to him.

Eddie already had the respect of the young people because he had been brought up with their Mums and Dads. He did not fit into the young people's image of what a Christian should be like. He was not a Bible-bashing, posh, university-type Christian goody-goody. He was one of them. There was something in his rawness that was able to reach them, which had not been a part of my training as a vicar.

It was in order to answer the question of how a middle-class church environment could relate to an unchurched working-class environment that we ad-dressed our differences. The working-class and middle-class cultures, in which we were brought up, had different psyches. Both cultures needed to understand each other.

When I talked about being patient and forgiving people, it was as much to do with my upbringing as it was to do with my belief in Christ. My background had trained me to turn the other cheek and behave well. It is easier to do this when you have never had to worry about where your next meal is coming from. In my world, forgiveness meant acceptance of situations; in Eddie's world, forgiveness is weakness. In my world anger is indignation; in Eddie's world, anger is instinct – you need to be angry to survive.

It can be very difficult to reconcile different understandings of Jesus' teachings. Eddie and I knew that. But if we, with the benefit of all the time that we spent together, could not work out a common perspective on the Christian faith, how could we expect anyone else to do so?

Our different perspectives became a strength to the work that we did. If anyone criticized me for not being from Bermondsey, I pointed to Eddie who was Bermondsey born and bred. If anyone criticized Eddie for not being a Christian long enough to lead the service, he pointed to me, a Christian for twenty years and ordained in the Church of England.

Eddie and I were both proud of our roots but we felt no pride in the labels that called one working-class and the other middle-class. In Christ these labels are disgusting and to be abhorred because they create division and can keep us apart. However, we needed to use the labels and recognize and work with the division in order to overcome it and find common ground.

You do not need to be an expert in sociology to recognize the reality of the class structure. I am a middle-class man living in a working-class environment. When I get my hair cut shorter than short with a number two blade all over, I get praised by people with a working-class system of thought and criticized by people with a middle-class system of thought: 'Very nice, very clean', says the working-class person. 'It looks awful', says the middle-class person.

Eddie is a working-class man married into a middle-class family. He pronounces his Ts in Surrey but not in Bermondsey. Swearing is a bigger issue in a middle-class system of thinking. Eddie and I drive through the Elephant and Castle area of London. A taxi cuts us up. Eddie yells at him. I sit politely and say nothing. Same incident – opposite reactions. It is a cultural and not a moral difference.

The division is there in the names that people choose for their babies: Sharon, Tracey, Samantha, Ronnie for the working-class parents; William, Kate, Elizabeth, Harry for the middle-class parents. We need to recognize the reality of these divisions before we can rise above them. If we see the trip-wire, we can step over it. The class issue is a hidden trip-wire that can shatter the work that the church is doing, because it creates fragmentation, misunderstanding and division.

Money creates division. It is harder for a rich man to get into heaven than for a camel to get through the eye of a needle. A church in a working-class area might pray for a thousand pounds to repair their old church building and not get the money they want. Five miles down the road, a church in a middle-class area might pray for one million, five hundred thousand pounds to build a new church and get the whole lot. It does not mean that the middle-class church has one million five hundred thousand times more faith than the working-class church; it means that the middle-class church has more access to money.

In the same way that Eddie and I had to work through the issue of class, Dave, who was black and was helping us with the service, and Eddie had to work through the issue of black people and white people working together. Dave and Eddie became the epitome of black and white. They had a shared set of understandings and prejudices against each other. Eddie had been conditioned by his environment to distrust black people. Dave had been conditioned by his environment to distrust white people. The developing relationship between them became an important part of the work that we were doing. It was hard work to reconcile these differences but it needed doing.

Dave got involved in the work after becoming a Christian through a dream. In the dream he was trapped in a fire and was terrified. A figure appeared and led him out of the fire to safety. He knew, somehow, that the figure was Jesus. The dream convicted him of the reality of Jesus. Dave went back to Michelle, his girlfriend, and told her. She was challenged by what had happened, and later prayed and committed her life to Jesus as well. The first that we knew about what had happened was when they turned up at church – converted, committed and ready for action. They did not know whether St James', Bermondsey was Roman Catholic, Church of England or whatever. All they cared about was the fact that God wanted them there.

Dave was a strong character with a powerful presence and a vibrant sense of energy and enthusiasm, plus a vision for doing work for God on the streets of Bermondsey. He wanted to get out there and talk about God with anyone that would listen. Eddie and Dave were rattling the young people and challenging them to become Christians.

Dave was a black man living in white-controlled Bermondsey. Not only was he black but his girlfriend Michelle was white and blonde and beautiful. A black man going out with a white girl was 'totally unacceptable' to many of the white people in Bermondsey. One of the young women from the youth club at CUM beat up a friend of hers simply because she was hanging around with a group of black people.

Bermondsey is an area notorious for racism. At the

last general election, Southwark was the only con-
stituency to field both a National Front and a British
National Party candidate. Racism boils down to traditional inbred ignorance, however, rather than personal
hatred. The majority of white kids in Bermondsey have
black friends whom they treat with respect but if they
see a black man that they do not know walking along
the street there would be an underlying tension, an
awareness of his colour as a threat.

When I prayed for Dave and Eddie, I felt as if the two
of them represented Bermondsey. They came from an
environment that kept black and white separate and it
required a conscious effort to cross this divide and set
an example for the young people. If they could see
Dave and Eddie, as converted and committed
Christians making the effort to heal inbred prejudices,
they would then be in a position to recognize their own
ignorance over racism and start sorting the issue out
for themselves. With all three of us representing such
different upbringings and perspectives yet all agreeing
on the simple point of Jesus – it made the teaching very
powerful.

We taught the young people that knowing Jesus was
about Monday, Tuesday, Wednesday, Thursday, Friday,
Saturday and not about what happened for an hour in
church on Sundays. We did not want to create a high
tech rave service that people would then become
dependent on for their relationship with Jesus.

Jesus did not say, 'Meet me down at the synagogue at
nine o'clock on Saturday morning and we can talk
about God then.' He said, 'Come and follow me ...
now!' We were not taking out the need for church but
we were teaching the young people that the most
important thing was their one-to-one independent relationship with God.

Arthur is in Tesco doing his shopping. Jesus says,
'Hello, Arthur, you forgot the deodorant.' Arthur
ignores him. He is walking down the road with his

shopping. Jesus says, 'Those bags look heavy.' Arthur ignores him and carries on walking. He is at home preparing his meal. Jesus says, 'Mm, that smells nice, Arthur.' Arthur says nothing. He is washing up. Jesus says, 'Hard work this washing up, isn't it, Arthur?' He ignores him.

Arthur puts on his suit and goes to church on a Sunday. When he is in the church, Jesus says, 'Hello, Arthur, how are you?' Arthur says, 'Hello, Jesus, nice to see you.' Jesus says, 'Why do you speak to me today? I have been talking to you all week and you have ignored me.'

God created us and the most natural thing that he gave us was himself. Worshipping God is the most natural thing in the world and we have complicated it through rules and systems, messing up something beautiful. You only have to walk into a church to feel distinctions and differences oozing out of every prayer. Forget vicars putting on holy voices or cockneys putting on 'posh' accents when they pray. It has been going on for years. The church has been so successful in putting across the idea that when you pray you should be polite, respectable and well-behaved that young people, who have never been inside a church building, have somehow picked it up.

Eddie did a piece of drama at CUM about the temptation of Jesus in the desert. One young girl was playing the devil and another was playing God. Eddie played Jesus. Without any prompting the young girl playing the devil launched off in her own sharp, streetwise cockney accent and the young girl playing God spoke in a plummy voice. No one had told the young people how to play the parts. They had reached their own conclusions. Have we got God's message mixed up somewhere down the line?

A young person came into CUM to help with the session for the ten to thirteen age group. She saw someone hitting someone else. She grabbed hold of him, called over the person that he had been hitting and said, 'Go on; hit him back.' That is what she had learnt at home as the best way of dealing with a situation – give back like for like; someone hits you, so you need to hit them or else they will come back and hit you again. On another occasion an identical situation was handled differently. Jo kicked Steve; Steve went to kick him back but was pulled up by a Christian youth group leader. He was told that it was wrong to hit people. Steve was confused at what he had been told and was upset and frustrated that he had not been allowed to stand up for himself. When his Mum came to pick him up she asked what was wrong. When he told her, she said, 'You mean that you didn't get him back? You fool!' and clouted him round the back of the head.

Pulling Steve up and telling him not to hit back did not teach him anything about Jesus. It left him confused because it contradicted what he had been told at home and what his environment had dictated to him. 'Turn the other cheek' has different connotations in an environment where you are actively taught to hit back. I needed to be careful that I was teaching the kids about Christ rather than teaching them a respectable code of conduct.

One of the Christian helpers was talking to the young people about smoking. He said that Christians did not smoke. Half of the young people listening to him smoked. Did this mean that they could not become Christians? In that Christian's independent relationship with God he might have come to the conclusion for himself that it was wrong to smoke. When he started saying that Christians should not smoke then he was putting obstacles in the way of young people becoming Christians. Was he talking about Christianity or was he talking about his own respectable code of conduct?

Gemma and Carly, aged twelve and ten, knew the

answer to this. As far as they were concerned he was talking about a respectable code of conduct. They thought that Christianity was 'posh'. Why should they want to become 'posh', so why should they want to become Christians?

Why is it that I spend five minutes at the beginning of every conversation, each time I meet someone new, breaking down their illusions about what a vicar does or does not think or do? 'You are a vicar – does that mean you are not allowed to drink? ... Does that mean you are not allowed to swear? ... Does that mean that you are not allowed to have sex?'

People have an idea of what a postman or a lawyer or a TV presenter does. Why do they have so little idea about what it means to be a vicar? Are the people that I meet particularly stupid or have we been putting across the wrong message?

Why does Gemma think that Christianity is 'posh'? Is she stupid? Could she have a point? Is this what we have let Christianity become? There were two verses that Eddie and I found helpful in relating the Bible to the young people. The young people got angry. Bermondsey has an aggressive culture and people need to stand up for themselves. It can be the survival of the fittest; survival is fighting back and to fight back you have to be angry. We looked in the Bible and found anger dealt with in, for example, Psalm 137. The psalmist is in exile. Jerusalem is in ruins and the temple is destroyed: 'How shall we sing the Lord's song in a strange land?' (Psalm 137.4).

At the end of the psalm the psalmist is overcome by feelings of anger at what has happened to him and he says that he would like to take the children of the Babylonians and dash their heads against the rocks (Psalm 137.9). He is being honest. It is a 'they are my enemies and I hate them' type of mentality. It is gutsy; it is straightforward and real. We have all felt like that at some time or other.

So why does the Alternative Service Book, authorized for use in the Church of England, print the last three verses of the psalm in brackets, indicating that they can be left out when the psalm is read in church? Is it because the idea of taking the little ones and dashing their heads against the stones does not fit the unwritten code of conduct about how Christians should think or behave? This timid, safe thinking of the Church rips the guts out of the Christian message by trying to make it respectable and not allowing the different verses in the Bible to speak for themselves.

If we are angry, and both Eddie and I are angry, it is because the issue of middle class and working class does not only affect the accents that people put on when they pray in church. It does not only affect the amount of money that one church has and another church does not have. It affects the very interpretation of the gospel message that we are preaching as being good news for the young people.

Another example of where the interpretation usually made by the church made our job of relating to the kids harder was where Jesus says, 'If anyone comes to me and does not hate his father and his mother, his wife and children, his brothers and his sisters – yes, even his own life – he cannot be my disciple' (Luke 14.26).

Christians read this verse and find it embarrassing. They try to think of one hundred reasons why when Jesus uses the word 'hate', he does not actually mean 'hate'. Feeling embarrassed about certain things said by Jesus that do not fit into our nice safe interpretation means that we have lost our nerve, and if we lose our nerve, then we emasculate the Bible message. We lose the grit and power of Jesus' message and we lose the spontaneity of the Spirit. What embarrassed Christians in the church interested the pre-non Christian young people.

We talked about the story of Jesus on the cross. We

wondered whether the reason that Jesus said, 'Father, forgive them' (Luke 23.34) rather than 'I forgive you' was because at that point he found it hard to forgive them himself and so appealed to God. It was a thought that they could understand and by shaking the crucifixion story free of rigidly pious interpretations we could bring the story alive.

There is nothing respectable about the Christian story. Mary became pregnant before she married Joseph. The first person into heaven was a thief. We needed to be careful that we did not make the Christian message nice and respectable because it is anything but that and if we allowed the Christian message to become respectable then we put artificial barriers in the way of young people becoming Christians.

We as Christians have sat in church for so long and heard the stories so many times that our ears have become dulled and the stories have become fossilized in our minds. Easter and Christmas have become part of the yearly routine rather than a part of the dynamic of how Christians tell their story. The Christmas story is sentimentalized and the Easter story is trivialized out of existence. Is Christmas about Father Christmas going 'Ho, ho, ho', angels singing and lambs being born in the middle of winter? What about the fear that Mary would have felt at having to tell her fiancé that she was pregnant and that it was not his child? What about the anger that Joseph would have felt? What about the sheer brutality of all the children aged one year and below being killed at the orders of Herod? How many times have we heard the story of Herod killing all the children and marvelled at the escape of Jesus, rather than shuddered at the horror of the killings?

The Easter story is about little chicks, hot cross buns and chocolate eggs. What about nails through someone's feet, crunching bones and sweating blood? The celebration is important, but if Easter is reduced to no more than that then it is not real. We hear the stories so often that we forget how dramatic they are. If people hear words used often enough, they get dulled to their meanings.

We might picture the Good Shepherd as tall, handsome and blond, disappearing into the sunset to find the sheep that was lost. Richard, one of the young people, thought that the shepherd was a 'tight git' for leaving the ninety-nine sheep on their own and searching for just one. The young people saw Jesus as 'shitting himself with fear' in the Garden of Gethsemane. They saw Joseph thinking that it was a 'liberty' for Mary to be pregnant and the idea that Mary might have been made pregnant by the Holy Spirit was 'macca'. (In cockney rhyming slang, macaroni rhymes with pony ... pony and trap ... crap.)

When the young people listened to the Bible stories and interpreted them for themselves, the stories came alive and they were fascinated. If we had cloaked the stories round with the interpretations that had been worked out already, we would have killed their interest and destroyed the significance of what we were telling them.

What about Jesus saying that we need to become like little children in order to enter into the kingdom of heaven (Matthew 18.3)? The child that Jesus is referring to is always assumed to be a well-behaved, passive-mannered, sweet-tempered kid listening to what his parents are saying with wide and adoring eyes. In other words, the child is understood as someone that Gemma would consider to be 'posh'.

What about Jacob, who held on to his brother Esau's foot in the womb because he wanted to be the first out and later cheated to get Esau's birthright for himself? Was Jacob the type of child that Jesus was referring to when he talked about needing to become like little children? It was Jacob, and not Esau, who got his father's blessing and was used by God because he was the hungrier of the two brothers.

Take all the issues that have concerned the church over the last few years – ordination of women, homosexual priests, the Church Commissioners losing hundreds of millions of pounds – and add up all the emotions and heartache and betrayal and hurt caused by these issues. The end result is something that is still not as important as the fact that we are putting across a picture of Jesus that Gemma considers to be 'posh'. In doing this, barriers are placed in the way of her getting to know Jesus Christ. It is as if we, in the church, have been arguing over the family silver and in doing this we have lost the one heirloom of any real value or significance.

Jesus says that it would be better for us to drown, dragged down to the bottom of the sea with a millstone round our neck, than to give out messages that put young people like Gemma off Christianity (Luke 17.1-2).

10
Mistakes and Conclusions

I pass over with silence, how without all fruit, yea with how terrible ignorance the lay and unlearned people say the pater noster and also the creed in the Latin tongue.

(William Tyndale)

A friend of mine, who is an artist, said that when she was not sure of what to paint she would put any colour on to a piece of paper. Once she had put that colour on to the paper she would put another colour next to it and so on until she had built up a picture. The work that we did was littered with mistakes but we needed to make these mistakes, in order to build up a picture of what we should be doing. If we had not been prepared to make mistakes and to learn from the mistakes that we made, we would never have started anything.

'If something in God is worth doing, then it is worth doing badly' – in other words, if it is worth doing, get on and do it and God will pick up on what you do and will take you to where he wants you to go. We wanted the kids to get to know Jesus and if we tripped up on the way, that was not going to stop us trying again. 'If at first you don't succeed, fail, fail and fail again.'

We made mistakes because the whole thing got out of hand. There were people all around us demanding our attention. There were Christians, who wanted to be taught about God. When we started the services we had Sunday after Sunday full of bright and attractive worship that had left Eddie and me, in the middle, feeling exhausted. Once the young people started to come into church, the people who had previously come for a bit of worship were now leaving, stressed out by the young people.

There were the Parochial Church Council (PCC) meetings, when people in the church were becoming interested in what we were doing and needed explanations about the burst of energy and activity around the church on Sunday evenings. The early evening Holy Communion service, which happened a couple of hours before our service, had been transformed from a quiet occasion when people could come and have 'oasis time' with God into a situation where those arriving for the service had to run the gauntlet of young people hanging around waiting for their service to start.

We had young people and we were bringing them to Christ. They were standing up in church, saying that they wanted to be Christians and that they wanted to commit their lives to God. We did not know what to do and we were not equipped for the extra work that needed to be done when they became Christians.

Paul was a Scottish lad, recently arrived in London and a heroin user, among other problems. He said that he wanted to become a Christian. He even com-mitted his life to Christ. We were not sure how to handle the situation, as he was homeless. He was living on the street and so if all we had said was 'Thank you for committing your life to Christ; see you next week', he would have slept rough after he had spent a few days in Eddie's flat. I invited him back to my flat and for the next two or three nights we sat up until the early hours, talking about Christianity. We had good conversations. We were making progress. There is a lot of work involved in getting a pre-non Christian to understand what is meant by committing their life to Christ.

Unfortunately, during the day I was out at work and Paul was at home on his own. Temptation is temptation and he worked out that the home of a vicar was a perfect place to store stolen goods. He was no big-time thief but he stole bicycles. I was following the textbook method of the evangelist. However, my mistake was ignorance of the culture. I was ignorant and in my ignorance I was too trusting. I was not aware that Paul was out in the daytime stealing bicycles. When a person who had lost his bike heard that his and other people's bikes were being stolen and stored in the basement of the Cambridge University Mission, where I lived and worked, he was amazed. CUM had built up generations of goodwill in the community by working with young people and now, unknown to anyone at the centre, it was being used as a storehouse for stolen goods.

Eddie and I were going around in the middle of the chaos created by the service with great weights, too heavy for us, on our shoulders. For me it was new thoughts and spontaneity from the kids and pressure from the Christians. For Eddie it was the frustration and anger with the church and their lack of support. We would meet for prayer and talk for fifty-five minutes and pray for two minutes because we were so confused at what was happening. We were trying, without any great success, to keep up with everything. When the Sunday evening services had started, they had been 'nurturing' the Christians – both the original worship group and those who came to the service. Now, with the young people coming to church, the Sunday evenings were no longer giving the Christians what they needed so we would meet in the week in order to train and teach them. But what about the young people who were making commitments to Christ? They needed time and energy to talk through the Bible and understand what they had done.

This meant that we were involved in Sunday evening services until past eleven o'clock at night; we spent one night in the week teaching the Christians and one night a week teaching the kids – never mind the time that Eddie and I needed to pray together. It was all spiralling out of control. We had our own lives to live as well. Eddie was an actor looking for work and I was busy with the demands of my job as Director of the CUM youth centre. It felt like war and we were not ready for it.

We went through a period where all we knew was that we had to turn up at church on Sunday evenings. One weekend Eddie and Ali went up to Sheffield to her sister. They drove back specially for the service and as every mile on the motorway passed they felt more and more that they would rather have been doing anything else. I left Pippa, tucked up indoors, and walked across to the church, stressed out at the thought of the evening ahead. We were learning that trusting in God was a 'tough old game'.

There was a group of people from the church who were with us on Sunday evenings. They sang; they prayed; they talked with the kids; they wanted to see God at work. They listened when we talked about the Bible; they felt alternately excited, worried and alarmed by what was happening. They cleared up coffee chucked about the vestry; they mended doors when they were broken. They came to Weybridge on the weekend away with the kids; they dived into the river to save Rocky when his canoe had overturned and he could not get out from underneath; they had their glasses stolen, and raw beefburgers chucked at them in the middle of the night. The greatest mistake that I made in the two years that we worked together, from the start of the worship group to the close of the service, was to let this set of relationships slip.

Just as Eddie and Dave were brought together by God to work through the issue of black people and white people living together in Christ, Eddie and I were brought together to work through the middle class and working class issue. Now I think that Morag, the churchwarden at St James', who was involved in the work with the kids from the start, was brought together with me by God to work through the issue of how the PCC at St James' related to the work that we were doing with the kids. However, I became so fired up with Eddie by the need to get the kids to know Jesus that this became a blind spot.

We felt sure that what we were doing was God's work. Morag knew this. At one point, she actually said that she was glad for everything that had happened in her life because it all seemed to lead up to what we were all doing together. Morag was in a difficult position. She had a heart for the work with the young people but as a member of the PCC she was also aware of the concerns of the wider church.

What we were doing with the young people was so all-consuming that I began going back on things that I had taught and that I knew to be true. I had talked about the fact that if Billy Graham preached seven nights a week and each night that he preached a hundred people came to Christ, it would take about nine hundred years to convert the whole world. But if one person brought one other person to Christ in a year and the next year each of them brought one person to Christ, and so on, the whole world would be converted in about fifty years.

I knew that we needed to spend time with other Christians so that the evangelistic efforts were widened and carried by more pairs of shoulders than Eddie's and mine. However, Eddie and I could not sit down and give a blow by blow account to the other Christians of what we thought God might want that evening when sometimes there were young people running all over the church, shouting and screaming, or drunk and fighting outside. We felt that all of our energy and attention needed to be directed at the young people rather than the Christians. The Christians wanted us to explain to them what we wanted them to do. We wanted them to work it out for themselves as we were having to do ourselves and as we were teaching the young people to do.

We felt that the work was too urgent and too immediate to slow down to the pace at which the rest of the church were happy. Communication suffered because things happened so fast. We could not explain something that we did not fully understand ourselves. The church could not accept the need for a lack of structure and planning. We could not accept their concerns. By this time Eddie had lost his patience with the church and I was confused. What they saw as support for the work, we saw as destroying the spontaneity and freedom that had brought the kids into the church in the first place. This caused increasing pain, anger and frustration on both sides.

We began to feel that every minute we spent with a Christian was a minute less that we could spend with a pre-non Christian. It was the pre-non Christians who needed to hear about God rather than the Christians. The Christians were saved. We felt that doing anything other than evangelism was like rearranging the furniture in the bedroom while the house was on fire.

Eddie's vision was working with the young people, not Christians – that was my responsibility. I needed to keep talking and listening to the rest of the church and instead of doing this I began to take them, and the people who came along from the church to help, for granted. It was a bad mistake on my behalf – sorry, Morag; sorry, Adrian, Stuart, Pauline, Anne; and sorry, everyone else at St James', Bermondsey.

11

Conformity and Nonconformity, Systems and Spontaneity

Judge therefore, reader, whether the Pope with his church, whether their authority be above Scripture, whether all they teach without Scripture be equal with the Scripture, whether they have erred and not only whether they can ... Judge whether it be possible that any good should come out of their dumb ceremonies and sacraments into thy soul. Judge their penance, pilgrimages, pardons, purgatory, praying to posts, dumb blessings, dumb absolutions, their dumb pattering and howling, their dumb strange holy gestures, with all their dumb disguisings, their satisfactions and justifyings.

(William Tyndale)

Eddie and I went back to Weybridge along with Kirk and a group of young men from the service. Paul, a university graduate and a volunteer youth worker, had come with us. Kirk and Paul used some of the petty cash to buy some beers. The young people were drinking the beers and chatting up some women. Paul suddenly burst out, 'Receipts! We forgot to get any receipts for those beers. We need them in order to claim from our petty cash.'

Kirk crimsoned with embarrassment. He did not want to be thinking about receipts when there were 'birds' to impress. Later on Paul disappeared to do some shopping and Kirk bought some bread, pâté and some dried milk for lunch. He got receipts for all that he had bought.

'You can't buy that dried milk', said Paul when he returned.

'Why not?' said Kirk, rolling his eyes and wondering what he had done wrong now.

'Because it's made by Nestlé's and they sell powdered milk to Third World mothers which encourages them not to produce their own milk.'

'You what?'

Kirk was staggered At sixteen, he was interested in having a laugh and a giggle – something to drink, something to eat and a couple of 'birds' to impress. At twenty-three, Paul was concerned about Third World debts and receipts for petty cash. How could we ensure that Kirk did not end up annoying Paul and Paul did not end up confusing Kirk?

What is clear thinking to one person is confusion to another. What was conformity to people worshipping in church on Sunday morning was nonconformity to the young people worshipping God on Sunday evenings and vice versa. How could we bridge this difference?

We, the Christians, were the people with the message and therefore it was up to us to adapt that message. It was up to us to make God's philosophy real and accessible to the young people. This involved working through what were 'essentials' and what were 'negotiables' of Christian behaviour. Some issues were clear. We were not going to kill anyone, for example, or commit adultery, bear false witness or break any of the ten commandments. Other issues were not so clear and required us to use our discretion. There is not a party line about how Christians should respond to each and every situation.

When he was asked to reduce the law and the prophets to one sentence, St Augustine replied, 'Love God'. He was saying that the love of God was the only thing that defined what a Christian will or will not do or say. To assume that a Christian will always react in a certain way in a particular situation is a form of spiritual racism. It is no different to making generalizations about Irish people, Chinese people or black people.

Both Christians, Fiona Castle and C.S. Lewis responded very differently to the death of their partners. Fiona Castle has talked in public about the sense of God's love that she felt when her husband died of cancer. C.S. Lewis wrote the book *A Grief Observed* to chronicle his despair when his wife died. They both had their independent relationship with God and were being true to who they were in how they dealt with the situation.

C.S. Lewis was the foremost Christian apologist of his generation. If there was one person alive at the time who you could rely on to give a convincing and lucid explanation as to why it was wrong for a divorced person to remarry then it was he. What happened? Joy Davidman was in hospital with cancer and he loved her and married her, never mind the fact that she had been divorced. An independent relationship with God creates a spontaneity, which is the reality of the Christian faith.

There is a thin dividing line between a Christian subculture and a new life in Christ. A Christian subculture can develop when churches and other Christians suck a person into a pattern of activity – home groups, Bible studies, coffee mornings, flower rotas. There is a need for this activity but once the need becomes a pressure and a measuring stick of your commitment to Jesus, Christians end up seeing themselves as defined by what they do rather than who they are in Jesus. Do they hold the chalice at Holy Communion? Are they on the leadership team? Are they in church each Sunday? How often do activities define relationship with Christ rather than relationship with Christ defining activities?

The danger of a Christian subculture is that some Christians become so immersed in it that they cannot relate to anyone outside that culture. They do not even feel that they need to. Why is it that people get caught up with this subculture, in which behaviour is more important that belief, when ultimately there is nothing required of Christians except to believe that Jesus died to forgive our sins?

If I were given responsibility for the whole church establishment, I would tell all the vicars and church ministers and leaders to do nothing for three years except preach about grace and about what it means. I would want them to teach people in the church that nothing was expected of them other than following their calling from God. At the end of three years I would guarantee that half of the leaders and half of the people would have left because they felt that there was nothing for them to do. The half that remained, however, would be so fired up with a true grasp of God's grace that they would quickly bring other people to the faith.

Once, when working for 'Crisis at Christmas', I was sitting on the floor smoking a cigarette and was mistaken for a homeless person by a clean-cut earnest-faced young Christian volunteer at the shelter. He asked, 'Do you know Jesus Christ as your Lord and Saviour?' He had not even taken the trouble to ask me about myself and find out that I was training for ordination and not a homeless person at all. Exasperated at the rigidity of his approach, his lack of freedom and flexibility and his total lack of any sympathy or understanding for who I was, I replied, 'Yes, I do. Now get lost.'

It was not a conversation to be proud about. I was not very charitable, but then he was not very sensitive. He was caught up by the feeling that if he did not talk about Christ to at least one person while he was at the shelter, somehow he would have let himself down. He had been caught by a mentality of system and any spontaneity was squeezed out of him. We all need some form of system to our lives because we need to know what we are going to do with each day. Once a system becomes set in stone, however, it can destroy spontaneity.

The anger which Eddie felt and my confusion became an integral part of our work and was an example of spontaneity. As textbook Christians we are not supposed to get angry. Yet despite this, the Bible is littered with examples of anger. While the Bible warns us about anger (Ephesians 4.26) it does not forbid anger in the same way that it forbids worrying (Matthew 6.25) or adultery (Mark 10.19). There is a lot of anger and confusion in the Bible.

Jeremiah was one of the most 'screwed up' people in the history of the world. He cursed the person who brought the news of his birth to his father. He was devastated when Jerusalem was captured and the temple was destroyed. How would the old system of worshipping in the Jerusalem temple survive with the Israelites in exile and unable to get to the temple? He challenged God with anger and grief and frustration and through this was given a vision by God of a new covenant and a time when everyone would know God in their own hearts and would not need to go to the temple (Jeremiah 31.31).

When Jesus threw the traders out of the temple, he might have been frustrated with himself as well as angry with the people present. He knew that in a couple of days he would be on the cross with nails through his hands, flesh splitting and guts ripped out and yet everyone was quite oblivious to what was going to happen. The temple was a hive of activity with people quite unaware of what was about to take place. We believe that there is nothing greatly immoral about money trading in church buildings – every vicar and church leader who has preached on that passage must have had a jumble sale or a bookstall in their church at some time. Jesus overturning the tables was a cry of indignation against the moral laxity of the temple but also a plea for attention.

As soon as Jesus had kicked out the money traders he brought in blind and crippled people who shouted out his praises. 'Look, they understand. Why can't you?' After he walked out of the temple he saw a fig tree without any fruit and cursed it so that the tree withered and died. He was very wound up. He let his control slip and showed his frustration; something that made him more real to the young people.

Was Peter angry rather than frightened when he denied Jesus three times? Peter had said that he would never deny Jesus and in front of all the other disciples Jesus had delivered a massive put-down, saying that before the cock crowed Peter would deny Jesus three times.

Then in the Garden of Gethsemane, when they were surrounded by Roman soldiers, Peter drew his sword and was ready to fight. Again Jesus stopped him and told him to put away his sword. Jesus was taken away by the Roman soldiers and Peter sat in the courtyard outside – something akin to a French resistance fighter staying outside Nazi headquarters – hardly the actions of a frightened man. We saw Peter, when asked if he knew Jesus, replying angrily through clenched teeth, 'No, I did not know him.' In Peter's eyes Jesus had made his choices and deserved what he got. It was only when the cock crowed that he broke down in tears of remorse. It is a less sanitized interpretation than Peter being frightened and then crying tears of remorse when he realized what he had done, but it is an interpretation more relevant to the young people.

Kids smell you out if you are anything less than genuine. When the young people meet you they push you and push you and push you in order to work out what they can expect from you. Authority is nothing; respect is everything. Once you are known and accepted then everything is 'sorted'; you could not be safer. Once I was known and accepted I knew that my car would be safe the next morning if I forgot to lock it.

Tyres of cars parked either side of mine have been let down while mine have been left alone.

Working with young people required a strong nerve. On one occasion when I lost my nerve, Eddie helped me recover it by making me lose my temper. Some of the young people had staged a sit-in in the minibus for a laugh, and had refused to move for some hours. Richard was the person in the group who was always trying to cause a laugh at other people's expense. He could be very funny and great company on his own. Sometimes he would take things too far. This was one of those occasions. He had taken a swing at me with a spanner. I felt badly flustered.

Eddie and I met to pray. I was full of Christian virtue and a macho 'Christian to the lions' type of humility. I was caught in the trap used by Christians who present the difficult situations that they have encountered as badges of honour, proving the good work that they are doing for God. I felt that this violence against me was something that I had to put up with: 'Accept. Love them as and where they are', and so on.'

'So what are you going to say when you see Richard?' asked Eddie.
'I don't know', I replied, full of reasonableness and acceptance and virtue.
'What are you going to say when you see him?' asked Eddie again.

He asked that one question over and over again. I began to get frustrated. I had work to do. I was preparing the club in CUM for the young people that night. Eddie followed me round, taking up my time, getting into my space and beginning to annoy me. 'Why give me stick?' I thought. 'I am the one who is hard done by. I am the one who deserves the sympathy.'

'So, what are you going to say when you see him?' asked Eddie. Finally, I cracked and wheeling round to face him, I shouted at him, 'When I see Richard I will tell him that he is wrong and out of order in what he did.' I felt very angry with Eddie. He just smiled. 'Then do it', he said.

I had thought that it would be wrong for me, as a Christian, to show Richard how angry and hurt I was by what he had done. It took Eddie forty-five minutes to break through this anaesthetic of textbook virtuous behaviour and enable me to stop leaving my own feelings behind and to escape from the concept of how I thought that a Christian should respond. When I saw Richard I was very angry over what had happened and he respected that in me.

Paul writes about becoming weak to the weak and being like someone under the law to those under the law in order to capture people's attention for Christ (1 Corinthians 9). The kids were outside the system and I was becoming like a person outside the system in order to reach them for Christ. One young person knocked on my door wanting his hand bandaged. His hand was badly cut. Pippa bandaged his hand.

'What happened?'
'I cut it on a window.'

Ask no questions! A group turned up at my flat before Christmas with a pair of cuff-links from a chain store.

'Happy Christmas, Bob.'
'Thanks.'

What was more important? Was it finding out whether the cuff-links were stolen, or accepting what the group were offering for what it was worth? What was going to be most help in getting them to know Jesus?

When presenting Jesus to Christians or to non-Christians the church is able to teach Christianity as a series of facts that are then understood by experience. Jesus died for your sins (fact). Commit your life to Christ (experience). This approach does not work for pre-non Christians because they do not know anything about Christianity. We needed to teach Christianity as an experience that would later be understood through facts. For example, pre-non Christians have no understanding of worship as a concept and so we did not try to drum one into them. It was only after they had been singing for some weeks that we explained to them that what they were already doing was worshipping God.

Experience had to go hand in hand with knowledge. Too much knowledge and not enough spontaneity would make them dry up. Too much impulse and spontaneity and not enough knowledge would make them blow up. Spontaneity with knowledge would help them grow up.

Some of the situations that we found ourselves in were fairly crazy as a result. When we took the group of young people away for the first time for a weekend we were staying on a remote river island in the Thames near Weybridge. Dave and Michelle disappeared during the afternoon to go to a gig in London. After the gig had finished they decided to drive down to Weybridge to join up with the rest of us. They arrived at three o'clock in the morning. The gates were locked. We had not expected them to return but they felt worried because we were on the island without a telephone. They had a mobile phone and thought that it would be a good idea to drive back and leave it with us. No one heard them calling and they decided to play a joke on the rest of us. They prowled around the campsite scuffling and pretending to be intruders.

Unknown to Dave and Michelle, a group of us had gone into town and had had a run-in with some of the local lads resulting in our group and the local lads shouting and screaming obscenities at each other. We managed to get them away before any fight developed. When we all heard the noise that Dave and Michelle were making we assumed that it was the local boys back for revenge. We were all gathered together in the one hut on the island. The more we heard the different noises that Dave and Michelle were making, the greater the tension became. People were ready with knives and coshes. I was scared. Eddie was torn in two. He was caught between his old life which talks of hitting out and fighting back, and his new life in Christ which hinted at something different.

The footsteps came closer and, closer to the door. We were all tense, ready for what was going to happen.

Bang ... bang ... bang ...

Dave knocked at the door and, throwing it open, stepped inside. Ricky threw a cross at him. He had made it earlier from two branches. It flew past Eddie and whacked Dave on the leg. In the split second before everyone piled in and attacked him, Dave cried out, 'Listen! What's happening?'

They recognized his voice. The girls were crying. Rocky – one of the more aggressive young people – fainted with fear. They were caught between pleasure and relief at seeing the two of them, and anger at what they had put them through.

Eddie was furious. He was angry with Dave and he was just as angry with himself. He knew that if necessary he would have hit out. He and Dave argued. Everyone was upset. In the corner some of the girls sat and began to pray and then sing choruses. It was three o'clock in the morning and they were doing something that we had never taught them to do. Quite instinctively, they were using prayer and praise to take the tension out of a situation.

Eddie had started a water fight and just as the night was turning and the grey streaks of dawn appearing, Gary woke up to find that someone had stuck chewing gum in his shoulder-length thick brown hair. Gary's hair was his pride and joy. He pulled out a sheath knife and ran round the camp-site threatening to kill whoever had done it. We lived three weeks in one night and ended up going back to London the next morning, too tired to think of staying any longer.

All of this was done in the name of Christ within

Eddie's original vision of promoting Christ to the young people. It made Christ accessible to them. Six or eight of them made crosses during the weekend. Why? They did not understand the cross and yet they were making crosses and relating it to what we are doing. One of the crosses was five feet long and was taken back and put up in the side-chapel of St James'. The battle was already half won. They knew that Jesus died on the cross. That was cemented in their minds, but they did not yet know why Jesus had died nor what that meant to them.

We encouraged the young people to develop their own experience of God and to work out their own understandings and definitions of God from what they experienced. This approach worked. Ricky tried talking to God and turned up for one service announcing with amazement that he had handed back some money when he had been given too much change. On another occasion he said, 'I keep finding pieces of litter and picking them up off the street.'

Some of the services we had with the kids were fairly wild. One evening, Eddie was at the front of the church playing his guitar and singing with a group of the young women: 'I believe in Jesus, I believe in Jesus.' Dave disappeared to the back of the church where he found a box of old clothes for the jumble sale. He came back dressed up like a pantomime dame and joined in the chorus: 'I believe that he's here now. I believe he is the Son of God.' One of the kids shouted, 'Blinding!' ('Brilliant!')

The rest of us disappeared to the back of the church. We all followed Dave's example and put on dresses and wigs and corsets and bras. We dressed up as women and to shrieks of hysterical laughter we pranced down the middle of the church, kicking our heels up in time to the music. Picture the scene: Dave who works out daily in the gym, Richard who is sixteen and large, myself the fourteen-stone prop forward, all dancing round the church singing songs of worship to God, outrageously dressed – crazy and mad, lovely and real.

When believing Christians meet to worship God the liturgy is used to express purpose and order and meaning. When pre-non Christian young people gather, the liturgy expresses chaos and disorder and mess and muddle. Why should and how can a young person be asked to make the conceptual leap into a liturgy of order and purpose when he may not know anything of that in his life?

We gave Richard a Bible to take away and read. He came back exclaiming with indignation and amazement, asking about 'this Noah geezer' who had, in his words, 'lived to be eight hundred and had kids when he was five hundred years old'. Richard had picked up the book and started to read it from the beginning. What were we meant to say? In order to read the Bible and to learn about God Richard needed a different environment from and different direction from someone who was familiar with the Christian stories. Richard was fascinated by Paul's resurrected and powerful Jesus. He had the traditional view that Christianity and religion and church were all about respectable manners and 'posh' people. Imagine his amazement when he heard a story about God throwing someone to the ground and blinding him. 'Is that what really happened?' he asked. 'Jesus laid Paul out?'

We do not do ourselves any favours if we picture Christianity like a holiday brochure, where the sun is shining and everyone is happy and enjoying themselves. It is not the glossy brochure view of God that appealed to Richard, but the violence of throwing someone to the ground and blinding him. Paul was off to kill Christians and God threw him to the ground and said, 'What is going on? Why are you persecuting me?'

Richard taught me about the reality of the story and about how I should relate other stories about Jesus to the young people. We could make Christianity more real to pre-non Christian young people if we did not mind showing them that a lot of Christianity confused us. To start with, I was nervous that they might ask questions to which I did not know the answers. I did my best to answer their questions but found that I was not helping. My answers were conceptual. They were not real to the young people. They were tying me up in knots. So instead I would say that I did not know the answer. As much as there is a human side of Jesus, there is also a supernatural side to him. All the greatest brains over the last two thousand years could not fully understand Jesus so what could we do in a few months? If we knew all the answers, we would be God. One of the kids asked Eddie

'How did Jesus put his hand on someone's head and heal him?'
'I don't know', Eddie replied.

This provided a real honest starting-point for the kids to think about Jesus for themselves.

What might confuse us could be instinct to a young person because whereas they live by impulse we are methodical and think before we act. There is a madness at the heart of Christianity that is summed up with a 33-year-old man nailed to a cross and dying in agony. It is not about everything being sorted out and in order. It is about brutal, bloody pain and confusion. Jesus begged God, sweating with fear and anxiety, not to have to go through with the crucifixion but still ended up on the cross.

We broke down preconceived notions of the church and we drew the young people into an understanding of God, which on a Sunday night for a couple of hours would turn their attention away from drugs and knives and pregnancy and prison. We found that in confusion God worked volumes. Men dressing up as women in the context of worshipping Jesus – so what!? On the next Sunday there were four, or perhaps even six, more people added to the service.

On another occasion Eddie and I were alone in the church with Alastair, a member of the leadership team. Alastair was painfully intelligent and methodical. Making a cup of tea was an issue for him because he knew so much about the volume of water and the construction of the tea bags that it blew his mind trying to keep all the information in his head. He had an IQ of about two thousand. He knew that God was somewhere in what we were doing but he could not work out where. He came along each week to the service. He was very faithful and determined to pray with us for all that we were doing. On this particular Sunday, none of the young people had come and we were on our own. Eddie was quietly singing to God. I joined in and we echoed each other's words:

> Father in heaven hear our prayer
> As we ask upon our bended knee
> Father in heaven hear our prayer
> Make tight our bonds to you and set us free.

Suddenly, Eddie's worship became a shout and sitting to sing and pray did not seem to be enough. I got up and started to walk around. Our singing became a shouting, a ferocious shouting. We were upset that no young people had come in. We were angry in our worship.

Our worship was totally contradictory to a textbook concept of Christian prayer. Alastair was amazed. What we were doing was raw and it was manic and in some eyes it could have been seen as contemptuous, but – we came close to God. It was a revelation to me because it was the only time that I had taken my most negative, most depressed, blackest feelings and had been able to express them in worship. I did not have to arrange my feelings or think about what I was saying to God. God had touched us and we were howling in anguish for God to bless the kids wherever they were. Afterwards

Eddie and I realized that we did not always have to give and that there were some times when we needed to receive. That evening was our time.

We got used to crazy things happening. Often, something powerful would happen in the service and we would walk out of the church and something destructive would have happened outside. On one occasion the kids were asking us how they could become Christians. They were telling us stories about how they were correcting their RE teachers at school, and about how they were telling their friends that they were coming to church, and they were asking us to give them Bibles to take home. When we went outside after the service, we found that Ali's car window had been broken and all her drama school gear taken. It had been a very Spirit-led and spontaneous service. By the next Sunday, the kids had found out who had broken the car window and had brought all the stuff back. The insurance paid for the window – the whole incident did not cost us a penny. After this sort of inci-dent had hap-pened a couple of times, instead of being angry we would praise God because we knew that we were doing his work. We were not surprised that whenever something powerful happened in the service, we would come out of the church to be met with some form of destruction. On another occasion we came out of the service and every plant in the park had been dug up and laid down in a circle outside the church door.

Confusion is an integral part of doing God's work. We developed a theology of chaos and spontaneity. It is two-dimensional theology to assume that when things are going well, then God's will is being done and when things are going badly, then God's will is not being done. We found that it was often in the chaos that God worked most powerfully. This was illustrated by the incident when Dave surprised us in the early hours of the morning at Weybridge. Amidst the confusion and chaos, the young women instinctively started to sing choruses and pray.

When I lived in India, a service took place on New Year's Eve to give thanks for the past year and to pray for the year to come. The church services were still heavily influenced by the culture of the missionaries who had set them up and were often more formal and English than evensong at Canterbury Cathedral. People would wear white shirts and dark suits, or carefully-starched dresses and sing nineteenth-century hymns with the organ thundering out in accompaniment.

On the stroke of midnight, just as the priest was about to begin the prayers for the new year, totally unexpectedly the doors opened and a rubbish collector walked in. The rubbish collectors scraped a living from the streets of the city by collecting large sacks of refuse for pitifully small amounts of money. They would walk the streets, dirty and alone, with backs bent as they hobbled along looking for discarded scraps of paper on the ground. The people in the church felt embarrassed and uneasy. They wondered whether he was mad and were unsure what he might do. He walked up to the altar, put his sack of rubbish down and prayed out loud a prayer of thanks to God for the last year. When he had finished his prayer, he picked up his sack of rubbish and walked out. It was an electric moment of reality.

Reality, immediacy, spontaneity were everything for the young people; images, pictures and actions were needed to capture their imagination. We acted out the parable of the banquet (Matthew 22.1-14) by putting on a massive feast in the church. We had wanted to invite everyone in the church to come to our service and meet the young people and celebrate the feast with us. We had invited the young people, their parents and anyone and everyone else. We had been planning the feast for weeks and in the morning service on the chosen day, totally unbeknown to us, the set reading for the week was the parable of the banquet. We took that as a confirmation from God that what we had planned for that evening was right. What we were not to know until afterwards was that by the end of the evening we would have re-enacted the whole parable in every detail. We used money that we had been given for this work by the Cliff Richard foundation and people chipped in with whatever they could afford. We ended up with £200 to spend on turkey and chicken and ham and crisps. To start with, we did not know whether we would have enough food but we ended up with enough for one hundred and fifty people to walk out of the church with their bellies full. We even had enough food to take the leftovers and give them to the homeless people living on the streets.

When we took a group out to do some shopping for the feast they could not believe that we had so much money to spend and that they could buy whatever they wanted. They kept on wanting to steal things and I kept on telling them that there was no need, and that we could buy it. The trip to the supermarket was an acted-out parable of the love of God. If the young people could not understand that if they wanted a bar of white chocolate they could have it by right and not steal it, then what chance did they have of working out that eternal life was theirs by right?

When the feast had got underway, the young people started to sneak sandwiches into their pockets and look around shiftily, wondering whether anyone was going to shout at them. They could not work out that the food was free and theirs for the taking. If they could not work this out then how were they going to work out the free gift that God had given to them in Jesus Christ?

The feast was a celebration of extravagance. The evening started mad and then got madder. We had a little service before everyone tucked into the food.

Dave drove round Bermondsey in his BMW shouting out to people that there was a feast at church and if they wanted some 'munchies', then they should pile in. I was at the front of the church taking the service and I kept on seeing Dave appear with another group of young people. He was going out into the 'highways and byways' bringing people to the feast. It was spontaneous and powerful and real. We had never seen the church so full.

We had a disastrous evening, however, on another occasion, when we tried to join together the believing Christians with the young people and have a joint service. We moved the service to an earlier time in order to join the two groups of people together. The young people were annoyed. They felt that they had lost their service in order to come to the grown-up service. 'Why couldn't they come to our service?' they grumbled.

During the service the young people behaved exactly as we had encouraged them and as they had grown used to behaving in their late evening service. If they wanted to walk about, they walked about. If they had something to say, they would say it. The Christians behaved exactly as they had learned to do and had grown used to behaving in their early evening service. They began to get tense and annoyed, thinking that the young people were showing a lack of respect. I was leading the service and was caught in the middle with the Christians on one side and the young people on the other.

I could feel the tension level rising among the Christians, and I could feel the confusion rising among the kids. We had been working for months to try and integrate them with the rest of the church and now that everyone was together at the same time, no one wanted it to happen. We were trying to fit the kids into a church structure. They were not ready for the structure and the Christians were not prepared for people who were not ready. Things got worse and worse. The young people felt unwanted and as a result began to play for attention. When the service finished all the Christians began to leave the church, as they were used to doing every Sunday. The young people were not ready because they were not used to having a formal finishing time. They began to get angry at being asked to leave and things then started to get out of hand. I ended up accidentally pushing Richard into a door as he made a burst to get back into the church once everyone else had left. It resulted in his head shattering the glass.

I went home feeling frustrated and furious. The confusion of the situation was illustrated by what happened once I got back to my flat. Church members felt worried for me and concerned for Pippa's and my safety because the kids were hanging around outside. They thought that the kids were angry with me – but in fact the kids wanted to ask me if I was all right and they wanted to talk about what had happened.

Why had we tried to join the two services together? Why did we assume that in order to get the young people to become Christians we would have to get them to church on Sunday morning with the other Christians?

It seemed an obvious thing to do. The idea that the gathered group of believers should be the focus of activity is a deeply-held part of the church's psyche. However, the assumption that linking the church with the young people and the young people with the church would do the job was too simple, neat, glib and packaged. We were not going to get the kids into God by trying to fit them into the system that we already had.

The kids thought that the normal Sunday church services were boring and irrelevant. We could have put a lot of time and energy into adapting the church services so that the kids would find them more interesting. Instead of this we wanted to create something new out of how the young people understood God,

The young people needed to be met where they were. They needed something that was about discovering, exploring, wondering, questioning. Sunday mornings were about receiving, listening, knowing and understanding. Church on Sunday mornings was not about complexity. It was the ideal. It was the utopia. It was good news to us because we were already saved and we already believed in God.

The young people might end up as church-going Christians but they were not going to start out that way. We would read the Bible through and, breaking it down line by line, we would explain it to them in a context that they would understand. 'Our Father, which art in heaven, hallowed be thy name' was translated as 'Hello, God. How are you doing? We love you.'

Eddie and the kids would meet me on Wednesday evenings in my flat and look at some of the Bible stories. The young people would wait round the corner, not wanting to be the first person to come in for a Bible study. We would do extemporary pieces of drama about, for example, what Jesus felt like in the Garden of Gethsemane. People would sit all the way up the stairs, and sprawl all over the chairs, smoking cigarettes and laughing. Richard would drive us mad by asking who this 'geezer' Adam was and don't we come from the apes anyhow?

The logic of the parable of the workers in the vineyard (Matthew 20) implies that someone can walk into church, having been a Christian for five minutes, and know just as much about God as someone who has been a Christian for twenty years. Jesus gave the disciples a child (Matthew 18) as a role model and a child cannot have listened to many sermons in church.

Jesus talked about the shepherd leaving the ninety-nine sheep to go and look for one that is lost (Matthew

18.12–13). What sort of church structure would be needed to allow for a minister who might not turn up on Sunday because he had gone to another church with a non-Christian friend? It would drive most people mad but those are the ideas laid down in the Bible and so those are the ideas with which we chose to work.

We felt that we were doing something right but at the same time we were really annoying some people. They felt that having cigarettes stubbed out in church, empty lager cans left around, tea bags thrown against the wall and sugar poured into the kettle was not what church was all about. They felt that the bad language and the smoking and the damage was deeply disrespectful to the church which was meant to be the house of God. They felt that we had lost control of what happened in the evening services and that the young people were not observing any 'boundaries'. What they said was true – we had deliberately never set boundaries to the behaviour of the young people. We were asked, in a letter from the vicar, to close the service down for a 'cooling-off' period. This would give people in the church an opportunity to assess what had happened and to decide on what might be done next and how the service might continue.

So we come to the night just before Christmas when Eddie, Ali and I were standing out in the rain with the service shut. There was an early evening Holy Communion which always took place two hours before our service. We had been told to come and tell the young people that their service was shut and to stand guard so that they did not come into the church and make a noise. The Christians going into church for their service were embarrassed at the spectacle of us standing out in the rain asking the young people not to come into the church. The young people shut outside were angry with us.

The young people had grown to look forward to coming to church. They had grown to trust Eddie and me and they were angry at the suddenness of the decision to close the service. They wanted to know why their service was being shut and the early evening service for the grown-ups was still going ahead. 'Why are you shutting our service? Why don't you shut the service for them?' they shouted, pointing at people going in for the earlier service.

It was miserable – winter, wet and cold. Eddie, Ali and I were soaked beyond caring. My socks were drenched, my shoes squelched, my underpants were saturated, my jeans heavy with water. My face, hair, shirt, coat were all soaked. I felt too dispirited even to shelter. I sat outside the church with the drizzle of the winter's evening running down my hair and down the back of my neck. I could have jumped into a swimming-pool and would not have got any wetter. My teeth were beginning to chatter with the cold but I felt too lethargic and lifeless to care.

Eddie felt terribly betrayed and his anger and frustration towards the church increased even more. He was pacing up and down outside the church, too restless to keep still. Ali stood quietly by the door, confused by all that was happening.

It was one of the worst nights of our lives. We felt cheated, compromised and crushed. We felt that we had let the young people down; I felt that we had let the rest of the church down; but worse than that, we had let ourselves and God down. 'Let's barricade ourselves in the church!' Eddie said. 'Let them physically remove us from the church.'

We did not do this. To the strong objection of Eddie we submitted to the authority of the decision and cancelled the service that evening as had been requested. We arranged a series of meetings with church members to discuss how the work with the young people could continue alongside the rest of the life of the church.

Eddie, Ali and I, together with people from the

church, discussed 'boundaries' on smoking and drinking and swearing. We discussed opening and closing times. We took the spontaneity of the services and tried to make them fit into the existing structure of the church. We had long and tiring meetings in order to try and forge an agreement over how the service might continue. Three A4 pages full of rules were drawn up. Our services had been rough and ready. They had started when they had started and they had finished when they had finished. They had been loud, unruly, exciting and creative. They had not-fitted into any systems but they had been saving souls. We submitted to authority, worked at getting into unity with other believers, prayed, fasted, hoped, believed. Yet, as we did this, we were killing the animal that God had created. When we opened the church again to the young people after Christmas, no one came.

12

Four o'clock in the Morning at the Crunchy Frog

> We will stand or fall on the conviction that God wants us
> to start the service again and to make him known to the
> young people in Bermondsey. We are convinced that
> there is nothing so significant for the church in England
> to face up to as the challenges and opportunities of relat-
> ing to pre-non Christianity.
>
> *(Eddie Webber and Bob Mayo)*

Our ways separated a year after the closing of the
service when Eddie got a part in a play about the Kray
twins and went off to Edinburgh. I stayed to work out
my contract at CUM. We joined up again when my
contract had finished and Eddie gave me a job in the
Crunchy Frog, a pub in Bermondsey owned by Eddie's
family. I had another job lined up as chaplain at South
Bank University but that was not due to start for a few
months. For a period, the Crunchy Frog was the only
pub in Bermondsey that could boast a 'vicar' behind
the bar. We were back in action, carrying on the work
of God.

One person in the pub came up to me with foam in
his mouth from snorting cocaine. 'Are you a vicar?' he
said. I nodded. 'Well, bless me then.' I said a blessing
and he went back to his mates, happy.

Eddie and I had not planned to work together but
here we were in a totally different environment,
meeting the young people with whom we had worked

in the church service, who were now coming into the pub to drink.

Eddie would look and listen and talk. On one occasion he sensed a group of people feeling uneasy about two people standing at the bar, who were obviously strangers to the area.

'Excuse me', he said to the group. 'Could you let me know before you clump those two over there?' They looked at him, astonished. How had he read their thoughts and guessed what they were thinking? Eddie then went up to the two men at the bar. 'Excuse me', he said. 'Are you two police officers?'

They were not the police and Eddie let people know. Everyone relaxed. It was a short, simple incident that took no more than a couple of minutes. Eddie and I were again absorbed in a pre-non Christian world, able to understand what was happening and able to respond. It made us realize the importance of what we were doing in the pub.

Jo, one of the young people who had been involved in the service, came into the pub and talked with Eddie. He told Eddie that the rest of the lads were saying that Eddie and I were no longer Christians because we were working behind the bar at the Crunchy Frog. He still had a blinkered view of what Christians should or should not do. He still had not grasped the spontaneity of God and he did not recognize that we were doing God's work in the pub.

He told Eddie that he thought that our place was back in the church. 'I always pray', he said. 'I always think of what you and Bob taught us ... Start the service up again; we'll come along. All we're doing now is hanging around the block of flats. We've got nothing to do and we talk about the service the whole time.'

We thought about what Jo said. He was right. We need to get going again. The work has not finished. It has only just begun.

Postscript

It does not seem as if the service will ever be able to start again. Eddie and I have been told that it is no longer possible for us to restart the service since we are now living outside the area. However, the work with the young people in Bermondsey still lies heavy on our hearts.

The Post-Evangelical
by Dave Tomlinson

A controversial book which should be read by every person disaffected by their experience of evangelicalism – and by every evangelical leader. It raises vital pastoral and theological issues, within a biblically-based framework, and highlights the agenda facing Christians at the close of the twentieth century.

Bread of Life
Stories of radical mission

Ronald Sider tells the stories of ten ministries around the world that combine social action and evangelism in a radical agenda, bringing Kingdom values into the lives of ordinary people. Included are the stories behind Steve Chalke's Oasis Trust, and Roger and Faith Forster and the Ichthus Fellowship.

Members Only?
Is the church becoming too exclusive?

This entertaining and revealing book gives a unique glimpse of the Church of England. Backed up by a specially commissioned survey, former BBC Religious Affairs correspondent Ted Harrison looks at the *real* attitudes of clergy and people towards the vital question of whether the church has become no more than an exclusive club, no longer providing ministry for all.